THE COUNTRY OF WHITE CLOVER

One of H. E. Bates' wonderful evocations of country life, this is a celebration of joy in earth, air and sun, of delight in the loveliness of seasonal changes, as experienced by the mind, the heart and the senses. It abounds in deep and pungent thought on country ways, an abiding love of the French countryside, and in sensuous delight in all that places country life among the richest of experiences.

THE COUNTRY OF
WHITE CLOVER

To

R. L.

THE COUNTRY OF WHITE CLOVER

by

H. E. Bates

Magna Large Print Books
Long Preston, North Yorkshire,
BD23 4ND, England.

British Library Cataloguing in Publication Data.

Bates, H. E.
    The country of white clover.

    A catalogue record of this book is
    available from the British Library

    ISBN 0-7505-1663-1

First published in Great Britain by Michael Joseph Ltd., 1952

Cover illustration © Sharon Stiles by arrangement with
Swift Imagery

The moral right of the author has been asserted

Published in Large Print 2001 by arrangement with
Evensford Productions Ltd., care of Laurence Pollinger Ltd.

Magna Large Print is an imprint of Library Magna Books Ltd.

Printed and bound in Great Britain by
T.J. (International) Ltd., Cornwall, PL28 8RW

Contents

Contents

1 *Journey to Spring*

We began to drive south through France in April, in what ought to have been spring-time, after the wettest winter Europe had known for eighty years. Wheat fields in Northern France, across the long switch-back countryside of the Pas de Calais, always so beautiful with ripe corn in mid-July, were simply lakes of glassy water pelted by sudden white squalls of hail and snow. Down long high avenues of elm and poplar occasional gangs of workmen were lopping, after the universal French fashion, every lateral bough from the tree-trunks, leaving them simply like black scaffold poles sprouting a few dismal boughs, like crow-scaring inside-out umbrellas, at the tops. There was not a single touch of green on them or indeed on anything else except an occasional hawthorn bush in the shelter of a hollow. At Beauvais we were glad, together with a number of other desolate travellers, to remain over lunch and its attendant and necessary coffee and brandy until nearly four o'clock, watching through the restaurant windows ghostly bits of sunlight running swiftly away before raw chasing rollers of cloud, black and then vicious white with spitting snow. It was not until we got to Paris that we saw, in a little suburban garden of otherwise unrelieved dismalness, in front of one of those shuttered grey-blue French houses that always look like abandoned signal boxes, tolerable only in the gaiety of summer, a small peach-tree. Its leafless branches, not much wider than a good-sized parasol, were dark pink with flower.

At Versailles and then again at Fontainebleau, through the long avenues of forest, the sun came out. Its colour was almost green, a sort of sharp golden green, in its late brilliance, and there were touches of green on hornbeams and hazels on the forest edge. A few white anemones were out and a man and a girl, bare-headed, arm-in-arm, were stepping delicately over puddles as they came up to the road from one of the long woodland paths. There was still no real greenness anywhere, except the late and lovely greenness, really a rare sort of gold, of the evening sunlight; but in the gardens about Fontainebleau a few more peach-trees were in flower, and on the roadsides further south, always against saturated and desolate fields, a few bushes of blackthorn. All the time the sky was clearing, less green and sharp and more golden and tender, until at last, at Sens, just before sunset, the whole evening was embalmed in a pale orange ripeness, under a cleared sky. But there too the streets were lakes of mud, like brown batter, and the night air was bitter as December.

Southward, in the morning, spring began. It came, first of all, in handfuls: at first hardly even in handfuls, only in fingerfuls, in a few sprigs, as it were, of roadside cowslips. I have never considered the blackthorn, even in fullest flower, as a tree of springtime. It is a bitter, comfortless sort of tree, a black widow left over from winter; and although all that morning, all down the wide valley of the Yonne, one of the most beautiful of France's many beautiful rivers, there were miles and miles of blackthorn in blossom, they did nothing to take away, for me, the old sour taste of a winter that had stayed too cold, too wet and too long. The countryside here is wide and full of meadows; and soon not only the roadsides but the meadows were yellow with cowslips, thick and sweet and trembling everywhere. There were miles and miles of cowslip fields. There were now also full leaves, almost flags of green, on some of the chestnuts, and even an occasional eye of green, pale as the cowslips stalks, on new-pruned vines standing like stunted knobs in still flooded furrows. But that morning, everywhere, it was really the cowslips, in their warm and golden millions, that brought spring flowing up to us from the south, blooming in air that was softening every hour until at Macon, where we lunched on the banks of the Saone, another exquisite river, the water of the stream was brilliant blue and the sun warm at last without treachery.

Hereabouts, as in so much of Central France, the country is wonderfully, almost painfully, like England. Hedgerows, little fields of pasture, straggling roads, shapely copses, cowslips and cows: nothing I have ever seen in Europe has quite the same nostalgic pattern of home. And it was here, on a scrubby hillside, rather like a hungry slope from the Berkshire or Sussex downs, that we saw, for the first and only time, what I had been looking out for. A few silvery purple groups of pasque flower, *Anemone pulsatilla*, like down-hanging silken bells, were growing among stunted cowslips in the chalk.

We came, that afternoon, into a countryside of peaches. I dozed a little in the car after lunch and woke, warm with sleep and sun, to see a landscape of long valleys, against blue-grey distances of mountain, on the sides of which countless orchards of peach-trees were smouldering in airy puffs of pink, some light, quite shell-like, some darker, with a brilliant raspberry rose. All the valleys south of Lyons were alight with these peach orchards under a lovely tender sky. Cherries were in blossom too: but never quite so startling or, for some reason, quite so endearing and delicious as the airy transparent peaches and the darker rose-bud nectarines. A few apples were beginning to show flower-buds and there were everywhere stronger breaks of green among the vines, but the cowslips had finished now, with the blackthorn, and here and there dark knots of maroon were breaking on lilac trees. Hawthorn everywhere was in vivid acid leaf and on the long avenues of plane-trees, especially about Orange, on the edge of Provence, there were breaks of palest, almost yellow green on the high bony branches.

The English, to their great impoverishment, have neglected the plane-tree. In England indeed there is a fixed belief, almost a tradition, that the plane-tree does not belong to the countryside and that it is exclusively, thanks to some peculiarity of constitution that enables it to resist the smoke and sulphur of London, a tree of the town. As a consequence London is full of plane-trees; whereas in the countryside there are practically none. France, on the other hand, has a million plane-trees. Prodigiously, with abandon, almost with joy, one feels, she has planted them everywhere: in streets, in squares, in market places but chiefly, and most liberally, on those long stretches of road that carve across France like great steel tape measures. And there, I think, they are probably at their most beautiful. The long lines of peeling grey-yellow trunks, capped in spring by buds of almost primrose green, darkened in summer by leaves of large cool friendliness, have a quality of dignity and refreshment given, I think, by no other tree. They seem to illustrate perfectly, too, the French notion of travel: that roads are for the simple pleasure of getting somewhere and that trees are for cheering and shading the traveller as he goes.

Occasionally the French vary their avenues of plane-trees with horse chestnut, and these were in full leaf, with a touch of flower, as we drove down beyond Avignon, into the dusty beauty of Provence, with its hillsides of wild mauve-grey rosemary, the following day. Here, for the first time, the soil was white and dry; dust was rising in the vineyards. Broom, thicker it seemed, more clotted and more richly yellow than our own, was sprouting everywhere from low hillsides of grey rock under pine and wild olive and, nearer the coast, forests of cork trees. Walnut-dark trunks, skinned of bark, squirmed knottily from grey scree and rock and shale that were graded off into still subtler tones of grey by bushes of wild rosemary and lavender and cistus and thyme. By afternoon the cistus, for the most part pink in flower, the kind of pink that is on the head of a matchstick, had finished their day. The large floppy rock-rose blossoms had dropped. But in the morning, in sun, they were in full glory: generally soft pink against grey, occasionally pure white, but smaller, against leaves of bottle green. And among them, even down to the edge of the roadside, large and airy anemones of purple and wine-pink and white, and then small irises – that is, small in height, but furling and flag-like in flower – of canary-yellow shot with purple, pale yellow with white, purple with cream, and pure white cross-veined with minutest stains of mauve. They clung to scree and rock and roadside with burnt white fists, spearing up dwarf lime-green leaves and flowers of orchid shapeliness: and sometimes among them torches of grape-hyacinths, powerfully blue, like threads of brilliant turquoise-black touched with a bloom of dust from the road.

Everywhere too, that day, wistarias were in bloom. They trailed over roadside cafés, on arbours, on trees, over farm walls. Farther north, even down to Avignon, they had been simply ropes of silken knots, almost colourless, hairy with down. Now they were spilling and climbing everywhere: strangling up eucalyptus trees, over cherry-trees heavy with small green fruit, over black cypresses. A touch of mistral, dusty and gusty rather than cold, had blown about Avignon and its cypress-barricaded fields, but southward from Aix, a delightful town of dignity and overpowering Martian plane-trees, the air lost all treachery, and with the change came the abounding wistarias, so rich and riotous, and the first roses.

By this time, nearing the coast, you could hear people complaining of the sad, long winter. Never, you could hear them say, was there a winter like this: no sun, only rain, every day rain, and all the gardens ruined. And then you saw roses, dark red, cherry-pink and that special tender peach-colour, just touched with gold, that is the glory of Provence, everywhere. Fat and crinkled, like stirred pink cream, they glowed on walls and pergolas and houses, and with them an occasional tree of pale yellow, a noisette sort of rose, a little paler and larger than the yellow jasmine that was blooming everywhere, over gateways and walls too and sometimes on the trunks of palms. A few late mimosas, of the long-leafed variety, were still in bloom; arum lilies were cool and lovely in the shade; solid streams of geranium and mesembryanthemum poured from rock and walls and peas were in full flower in the fields, where vines were sprouting tendrils – oh! the long, sad winter, with hardly any sun, and all the gardens ruined.

We drove on that afternoon through the burning brown gorges of the Estorel, smouldering under blue sky, and on through flat fields of carnations. The rocks were ferned with grey clumps of *cineraria*

19

maritima, in which park gardeners delight as they fashion their summer bedding. I had known and grown it often, never bothering to think about the *maritima* part of it; and now it was here, by the sea, true maritime, salt-coloured, another strayed sea-plant to set beside asparagus and seakale. It was a little flabby after winter, quite outshone by the rising nobility of aloes, flaunting already the most tremendous flower-shoots, like totem-poles. Their blue-grey leaves were exactly the colour of the sea but later that afternoon, as always, the sea took all the glory of the day, calming and softening down and in its smooth surface reflecting, in exquisite mixture, the blues, the greens, the pinks and the pale and changing coppers of dying sun.

Beyond the bays there were sudden revelations of shining snow. We drove up to them a few days later. A burst of heat in the great cup of hills about Grasse, where fields of lavender were growing, brought blue and pink anemones out like flaring stars under the olive-trees, and all up the slopes a million cistus were in flower, with rows of big common blue flags on the fringes of vineyards. We drove through formidable gorges of burnt sienna rock splashed with emerald broom and pine to reach the snows about noon. Up there little alpine villages, half in, half out of snow, had all the tawdriness of slums after the burial of winter. An odd skier was punting lazily through the upper pines, all alone, exactly as if looking for something he had lost far back in winter; girls in black ski-trousers were walking along streets that were furrows of water and brown-black snow. The great dreariness of thaw had settled in: sad, ugly, messy, a horrible left-over on a dirty plate. Not a scrap of beauty was anywhere visible until suddenly, on cleared patches of alpine grass, we saw the first crocuses. Pure white at first, exactly the colour of the fading snow, and then brilliant iris-mauve, strong and starry, they had the effect of many little lights on an earth made tawdry by thaw.

And then, a few moments afterwards, they were gone. There were no more of them, and we were suddenly down below the snow-line, in valleys half in winter, half in spring, among willows with yellow catkins and a few primroses by the waterside in the gorges below.

Only eleven days later we were coming north again. The riot of roses, the great festooning glories of wistaria and jasmine and pale blue plumbago had not simply richened; they too were travelling north. All spring was rushing up through France, in an immense sappy vivid surge of acid and tumbling leafiness. The Frenchman who spoke of the incomparable acid greens of England could never, I feel, have looked at his own country in spring. All the lushness of England in late Maytime, of olive oak flower splashed with wild cherry, of green-varnished poplars and floppy may-blossom, of meadows flaunting with buttercup: all of it was, if possible, more lush, more brilliant and more moving in the long wide valleys of

France as we drove home. And it was not only the brilliance and richness that was startling; the speed of its happening was a miracle. All the peach orchards about Lyons had finished their flowering and were in full leaf. As far north almost as Paris the cowslips had disappeared. Lilacs had joined wistarias to give luxurious shade to gardens that had been naked to sun as we first passed them. Dust was blowing in vineyards, all sparkling with fresh shoots, that had been flooded only a week or so before, and at noon it was too hot to eat in the sun.

And there, in the heat of a clear April morning in the countryside somewhere between Valence and Auxerre – Auxerre being only one of several superb and ancient French townships with the loveliest of water-fronts, and a wide river – I had the desire, as always at some time every spring, to stop the flow of it all and let it rest there. Nothing of later summer could ever, in any way, be more beautiful than this. The trembling and restless transience of the whole thing made the heart spring and turn over and ache with joy. In England more than half the beauty of spring is its length; its long four-month course draws out slowly, uncertainly, with repeated moments of exquisite and infuriating change. But here in France summer was folding over spring before spring had half unfolded itself. Plane-trees, naked as bone when we had driven south, were now giving thick and welcome street shade. And in front of houses women and girls were sitting out – infallible sign of French summer – on comfortless hard-wood chairs, knitting and gossiping and watching the world go by. All France south of Paris was brooding and basking and settling down like an old dreamy hen for summer.

The crown of all these delicious moments of feeling, heightened always by the fact that, in a car, you are drawing away, at sixty miles an hour, from the very thing you have been pursuing, came in the forest of

Fontainebleau. It is Paris' great good fortune that she possesses, within twenty minutes ride of the Arc de Triomphe, several forests of enchanting and ancient beauty, of which Fontainebleau is, even in that company, the loveliest. No man ought to die without seeing Fontainebleau on a warm spring day, with its magical avenues of tender leafy beech and catkined hornbeam and to hear, as I did, the heartbreaking chorus of countless nightingales. The whole world, composed utterly of green leaf and sun and scent of rising sap and involved and lovely choruses of bird song, seemed at that moment sufficiently and absolutely contained simply in what you felt and saw and heard there, shut in by green trees, under a cloudless April sky.

It was, as it turned out, almost the last of that early spring glory. Gradually, north of Paris, the trees went back to leaflessness. Spring, cool and difficult and slow, began to reveal itself again in sharp wintry bushes of blackthorn, an occasional peach-tree, daffodils in gardens and once more, now rather a belated joy, in cowslips by the roadside. The Pas de Calais, in parts utterly treeless, had the bald emptiness of a bull-dozed plain. Cowslips were tossed in cold wind among still dead grass and women waiting for buses, swathed in black shawls, in dreary little villages, turned their backs on gritty gusts of wind that would bring, by late afternoon, sad sea-mists from the north.

And in England the cuckoo, as always, unfailing, mocked us in a fall of snow.

2 The Country of White Clover

When I came to live in Kent twenty years ago, it was as an exile from a countryside of flat river plains, bland and broad and unexciting, across which the counterflow of the Industrial Revolution had left a red wash of brick streets whose common emblem was the aspidistra in the front-room window. I had lived, far too long, as I then reckoned it, to the sound of factory hooters marking the hours, the shriek of boot stitching machines in back alleys, the peculiar tangy odour of leather on wet and windless afternoons. Like D. H. Lawrence, I found it hard to bear the rape of central England by hands intent only on the spoils she gave. In so central a country as Northamptonshire, bounded by nine other counties, I had grown up also with a curious feeling of being shut in. Everything else of England, the sea especially, seemed far away. Excursions were necessary before I could discover for myself the simplest pieces of uncontaminated rural delight: the primrose woods of Bedfordshire, the cowslip fields of Huntingdon, the beech woods of Buckinghamshire. I was rather like a man brought up not only on the plainest of diets: for me it was bread and cheese at every meal every day. And I had begun to hunger, at last, and not unnaturally, for variation.

It did not occur to me for a long time after this that I had had the amazing fortune to discover every possible variation I needed within the boundaries of a single county. Kent is a large county: its astonishing range of qualities, born out of the happiest union of climate and soil and husbandry and sea, cannot be discovered in a day. It is also, virtually, an island. It is almost a kingdom. Two-thirds of its boundary are formed of water. The long sweep of the Thames from London Bridge to the Isle of Sheppey, the flat sands of Pegwell and the Goodwins, the vast creamy walls of cliff about Folkestone and Dover and the final oddity of Romney's strip of half-land, half-shore: all this has a curiously separating, isolating effect that to me, as a Midland man, has always been ceaselessly exhilarating and refreshing and beautiful and peculiar. If you can imagine Kent bordered on its seaward side, to the north and east and south, by counties having something of the characteristics of Picardy and the Pas de Calais you cannot fail to conclude, I think, that much of its distinction would have been lost. It would have become another rural appendage to London, simply another home county, half-suburban, insulated in fair comfort by surrounding counties taking away the first bristling and invigorating impact of sea. But the special arrangement of its geography precludes it for ever from becoming, for example, just another Hertfordshire. It remains intensely, sometimes infuriatingly, insular: a maritime county gaining more than half its character, its air and its beauty from the contact of sea.

To a man accustomed to making journeys of ten miles in order to gather the first primroses of spring it had, when I first came here, almost unbearably accessible beauties. Its primroses were cast everywhere on its roadsides; blue-bells grew in the hedgerows of its by-passes. Its woods had not been ravaged by the Industrial Revolution but remained, as they had so long been, the surviving segments of a great forest, on the sheltered clearances of which a snug fat husbandry prospered with extraordinary richness and variation. You could hardly walk a quarter of a mile without coming upon woods and copses of charm and lushness: yellow with hazel catkin in February, tawny-purple with alder caterpillars in April, foaming with sweet-chestnut in July. You were never out of sight of great trees. The quality of the land everywhere was of a startling fertility. The long ledge of sugary lightish soil running between the lower crest of downland and the dip to the Weald, a sort of great curved step running south-eastwards from Swanley through Maidstone and the sea, is one of the richest in the world. It supports a prodigious agriculture: to which aboriculture and horticulture have added a touch of balanced floridity and neatness that gives the whole county the name by which everyone knows it – the Garden of England.

Sea, hills, woods, marshes, rivers, parks, oast-houses, pastures, hop-fields, village greens, cornland, white clover, orchards – the incomparable, magnificent orchards – it is very hard to know where to begin in Kent. Sea and hills and woodland seem to me to dominate the scene. There is sometimes even a feeling, more especially on dull humid days of late summer, when the domination of trees, dark with too much rain, is almost too oppressive to bear. The horizons everywhere are unbearably shortened by masses of black leaf. A feeling that the sea is not only far away, but that it does not exist at all, dispels completely in these days the notion of the county being an island. It becomes again what it once was: a ponderous and undulating forest out of which man has fashioned, over the centuries, a few clearings for the cultivation of his corn, his apples and the most curious crop that surely ever climbed its way to heaven and big bank balances – the hop, that rustling, artificial-looking flower of green that drinkers for ever maintain, with stubborn sourness, is never to be found in their beer. So let it be said here, firmly and I hope finally, that that is what hops are for; beer is what they are grown for and it is into beer, incredible to the patrons of saloon bars as it may seem, that they go. As if Providence had not given Kent enough in the way of agricultural riches it gave the hop as a final measure.

On these dull oppressive days of late wet summers, before there is any touch of change in the leaf, and when the angle of light is beginning to lower a little, I feel greatly drawn to the sea. There is a piece of country beyond the final rim of downland, over towards Faversham and north-eastwards by Canterbury, where the land is high, with sudden gaps in beech woodlands revealing silvery distances of low estuaries and creeks on a far pale shore. Further north-westward you come upon sudden glimpses of the Medway, broadening out, populous with shipping, towards Sheppey and the sea. It is very much Dickens' country. He lived in it, wrote of it and, in some odd way, rather as a fire leaves a smoke-mark on the lip of a chimney, has left his seal on it. Rochester and some sections of shore and sea-port and countryside are his own as much as London is. A certain shabby, seedy, seaport fustiness, of the sort he loved to describe, remains about parts of Rochester, Sheerness and Gravesend, untouched by chain-stores and television poles. It is not hard to imagine some disportation with Pickwick, at Dingley Dell. Solicitors' offices, the offices of port

33

authorities with dusty gauze-covered windows, lace curtains over the windows of seedy Georgian boarding houses, squat rotund little pubs, the sudden discovery of upturned boats in back-yards: Victorian England, Dickens, the expansive and, as we like to think of it, prosperous and jolly times. Today a horrible general slatiness, a greyness as of abandoned ash-heaps, hangs over almost every yard of this north-eastern shoulder of the county. It appals by its dismal reckless pattern of slate and brick, of pre-fab and chain-store: another great back-yard of London, grey and dismal, composed of a million little back-yards, so raw and cancerous that it does not seem to belong to the rest of this bountiful countryside. Yet even here the great cherry orchards flower right up to the rim of the ash-heaps, just as they do about the hideous purlieus of Swanley, and in spring and summer the woods on the hills above Maidstone, only a mile or two before the destitution and decay sets in, are marvellously beautiful with white-beam and viburnum and wild cherry and traveller's-joy and all the many things that specially flourish in chalk hill-sides.

We are placed about centrally between this depraved and fascinating bit of river coastline, itself a series of islands, and the still odder island of Romney Marsh. At Appledore, only one of several enchanting forgotten and abandoned ports of which Kent is full, the land seems suddenly to pitch down to the level of the sea. Instantly the lush forestry of downland and ridge and orchard and even of Weald is finished; there are no more hops or cherries or sweet-chestnut copses or white fields of barley. The nobility of the great wool towns, Cranbrook and Tenterden, is replaced by small huddling villages with squat rose-roofed churches not much taller than the big yews in their church-yards. A remarkable little kingdom within a kingdom emerges, almost entirely of grass and water, with a population of sheep more dense than anywhere in the country: quite flat, green and curious, with a sky-line as far and wide as the sea. Herons poise with melancholy reflection on the long dykes, lovely with grey-lavender marsh-mallow and purple loose-strife in summer, grey-bearded with heads of reed in winter; kingfishers whistle with needle-sharp cries down a wide landscape that because of its emptiness gives a remarkably enlarged and bell-like quality to the smallest sound. A sensation that you are walking here on the bottom of a dried-up sea, a feeling perfectly correct in historical fact, increases as you go on towards the coastline. Tongues of shingle begin to cut into the dark green pastures, bringing in with them a range of sea-flowers. To the beauty of the mallowed dykes is added the dry brilliance of vipers' bugloss, vivid as delphiniums on shingle and sand in July, sea-thistle and convolvulus, yellow sea-poppy and foxglove. This fusion of marsh and shore, of land-flower and sea-flower, is of great beauty. It creates a curious air of being part of primeval things. To savour it is like going back in time, pushing away mapped and secure waters that we know well and accept as inviolate, and knowing suddenly what it is to see the sea-bed flower.

To the east of all this a new stretch of depravity begins. On this remarkable stretch of countryside, unique not only in its own county but in England, the forces in our lives known as planning authorities have allowed, over the years, the erection of a coastal strip of bungalows of astonishing hideousness, to which has now been added a holiday camp or two. The once-beautiful little village of Dymchurch, to which even in recent years misguided ladies have gone in search of quietness because they had once heard of its legendary charm as a little fishing village unspoilt on the edge of the sea, is now rather like a sample segment of the Mile End Road or better still, perhaps, Battersea Fun Fair. Its effects spread out for some miles along the sea-wall. Only New Romney, for some reason, has escaped them and remains, old, lost, dignified and quiet, perhaps the nicest town of the entire long coastline. Its short main street is perfect as an example, architecturally and atmospherically, of an eighteenth century seaport, now, of course, a port no longer, since the land is here, or hereabout, constantly advancing on the sea, pushing itself out at the point of Dungeness at the rate of some yards a year. Hideously the bungalows follow it. A mile or two eastward the sea revenges itself. Savagely, at Sandgate, the sea eats in, making the cruellest mockery of the works of man some dozens of times in the course of an English winter by hurling promenades and break-waters about as if they were flower-pots. Concrete is bashed and fissured like egg-shell and sea roads are blocked by barriers of shingle. Some eternally complex power of wind and current and tide is endlessly at work clawing lumps off land, pavements, houses and even, farther east still, the bastion of a castle.

Dover is out of reach of this merciless sea-beating. It is my favourite seaport in England: at first sight not impressive, rather drab, cruelly scarred by war, with a sky-line of dock-cranes not big enough to be important, a smell of coal-yards, a constant yawking and squealing of sea-gulls on chimney pots. Horrible gaps yawn in the semi-circle of its Regency sea-front crescent: half of which the local authorities have repaired and restored to decency, the other half of which they leave, for some reason, in monstrous decay. Its restoration could give Dover a crescent of maritime Regency architecture, perfectly set against a high background of hills, unequalled in England, a delicious curve of green and white fronting a harbour constantly tense with shipping, both steam and sail. The port indeed thumps with life. It contains in many ways the whole essence of Kent as a maritime county; all of the peculiar independence, stubbornness and restless-ness of this county, set so near to the continent and its potential invaders that it can never slacken into the sleepy smugness that comes over some ports of the west, is concentrated into this town with its superbly impressive situation. It is, of course, a garrisoned and fortified town: in that sense alone incomparable in England. Of its castle I will risk offending all Scotsmen by saying that it is as fine, as a specimen of permanently garrisoned fortification, as Edinburgh: perhaps finer. Seen from the sea, on a fine summer night, it stands up in the sky like some half-transparent model magically constructed of glass and salt and silver. By day it carries all the imponderable and invincible grimness, a sort of thundery and majestic cloud in stone, of the Middle Ages and of England defending itself over the centuries. It is, I think, even more than the cathedral at Canterbury, the symbol of the entire Anglo-Kentish character, the peculiar composite of suspicion, stubbornness, forthrightness and determination, all damnably annoying and yet infinitely English and admirable, from which love and fear of the sea are never absent. It reveals, more than any other English town I know, the salt in our blood.

You can even eat well in Dover. Its restaurants seem to have caught, by seaward rumour, a notion that there are countries where people may wish to eat after seven o'clock at night and even disport themselves, over wine, until the hour of eleven. They cater, as towns in England are apt not to do, for travellers: and at the most ancient of them, a sort of semi-ecclesiastical cellar called the Crypt, something as good as France can be found. Here, by a small miracle, in Dover itself, Dover soles may be eaten as they should be eaten: simply grilled or fried or Meunière, firm and white as snow, tasting like clean portions of solid sea. They come to the plate here as big as the shape of a giant's foot, yet never coarse, and in their best season, in winter, full of a rare delicacy. I mention this not merely to praise a restaurant, but because all along this coast, from the bay of Rye to the estuary of the Thames, the fish is unequalled in the world. From the shrimps of the Thames above Gravesend, where men still fish in their ancient bawley boats, down through Whitstable with its oysters and the reeking whelk-and-crab stalls of Ramsgate and Margate and Deal and Folkestone, on through Dover with its soles and finally round to Dymchurch and Rye with their famous plaice, the fish has the same first excellence as the fruit that grows inland. The Kentish sea, like the Kentish soil, is rich. Some fusion of coldness and current and food and perhaps high iodine content gives the flesh of flat fish here an amazing sea-salt flavour, sweet and yet tangy as seaweed and vigorous as the bluster of sea-air. It is sometimes possible to taste here an otherwise not very remarkable fish like halibut, in which the succulence of the flesh about the fins, glutinous and fatty, is like the essence of pure sea-foam. No visitor to the

Mediterranean should ever attempt the soles that are served there, laden with butter and almonds to give them flavour. He should save his money and go to Dover. There Kent will reward him – and if he loves oysters, as even Romans did, he is not much more than half an hour from Whitstable – with something of rare gastronomical beauty. He will feel that he is eating the sea.

Northwards from Dover the downs spread and break into a series of wooded folds. Beech-woods of high magnificence crown the innumerable rounded breasts of land that fill the countryside in the rough triangle composed of Ashford, Canterbury and Dover. Somewhere about here Caesar's invading armies made their camp. It is a piece of lost, steep-valleyed country, lovely and green: of abandoned great houses, scrubby little villages in twisted lanes that seem to double back on themselves and lead nowhere. Summer, giving long golden-green panoramas far over marsh and weald, is very beautiful here. Spring brings cow-slips on the short pale downland grass. Snow comes heavily in bad winters, filling the steep lanes like gullies, cutting off villages, burying sheep, giving weeks of isolation that are apt to cause surprise to persons dwelling on comfortable and snowless flat-lands below. This is the wildest, quietest and yet most uneasy of all Kent's countryside. Man has put less of his mark on it than perhaps anywhere else in the country, with consequences that are cold and peculiar. I am not ashamed to say that sometimes, on darkening afternoons, it frightens me a little. A touch of the primeval is left here, something of the old dark air that Cobbett caught and hated so much on lonely heaths as he rode about the south country in the eighteenth century, and I am always glad to leave it behind.

Everywhere these Downs have beauty and dominance. Without them, as without the sea, Kent would be reduced to ordinariness. They add something uplifting and fine to her already great pattern of variation and are themselves infinite in variation too. About Lenham they suddenly take on a remarkable starkness. Lenham itself is a village of extraordinarily French appearance, with a square exactly like those seen so often in France, with little rows of clipped and pleached shade-trees round the sides. Its neighbouring ridge of down is not so engaging. Its peculiar structure, acting like the stone slab of a waterfall, allows winds from the north-east to come sliding over the top with vicious bitterness, holding to the face of the bare precipitous curve exactly like a stream of icy water. Blizzards pile here with double the depth and force that they have in the valley of the Medway, only ten miles farther north, and snow lingers in deep drifts on roadsides long after primroses have begun to star the ditches of kindlier country. The Downs are really the bone and heart of Kent, just as the sea is the thing that gives it a certain headiness, a zest, of atmosphere. Constant conflict between sea-wind and these hills creates a maddening and yet invigorating insecurity of climate. The hills break the sea-cloud into intensely localized patches of rain. While sun shines on the flat coast strip about Hythe and Dymchurch, rain beats on the orchards of Sittingbourne; foggy cloud binds the Weald in rolls of cotton wool on an autumn morning, but the sky above Sevenoaks is all blue crystal and light, without a cloud. It is always the sea, with the hills, that confers these rapid changes on us here, saving us from the lethargy and enervation of the West. You feel here that the air is never settled, never stale or stable, never still. If indeed the weather changes here, as they say it does, with every tide, then we have only another reason for the curious and beautiful quality or freshness, almost a sort of sweet bristling, that I have noticed in the air here ever since I came down from the Midlands twenty years ago to live in a county that seemed fabulously fertile. It is a very sweet and pleasant air. I like it and I shall probably go on breathing it and liking it, I think, for the rest of my days.

This, then, is the country of white clover.

3 *A Piece of England*

Whenever I come home from abroad, more especially after journeys southward to meet the spring, it is less and less with Browning's nostalgic lines running through my head and exciting me. The virtue of being in England now that April's here, just because it is England and just because it is April, seems a more and more doubtful and mocking one. As I write, the month of April has already gone and I do not think there are many Englishmen, this year, certainly not I, who will wish to shed tears over its bitter parody of spring. If they seek any consolation in this it appears hardly likely that they are about to find it in the month of May. Bitterly and harshly, on this, the seventh day of it, a half-gale from the north-east roars in the black oak boughs; there is a great whistling and tossing in the half-opened leaves of willow and beech, and over everything sits an enormous colourless lid of cloud, dead and neutral, against which dark-boned trees shake and writhe with cold melancholy. There is not a sound of a cuckoo, a bird that I am convinced is becoming a rarer and rarer visitor to these shores every year, and not a note from the most delicious of May-time singers, the blackbird. All you can hear are occasionally a few brave twitterings, apparently more of fear than joy, half borne away by wind, and then the wind itself roaring wintrily in bare boughs. Here, at its wretchedest, is your northern spring for which poets have written their hearts out: backward, cruel, lightless, oppressive and, above all, stationary. It is like something pinned into a corner, cowering and shivering, held from any advancement by sheer paralysis. Even the country Jeremiahs, who at the slightest suspicion of an April temperature that rises one degree above fifty-five begin to wag smug prophetic heads and tell you 'We shall etta suffer for it, you see, you mark my words, we shall etta suffer,' are silent this year. They too are in their corners, shivering. Even they have had the heart knocked out of them, the will to prophesy killed, by a year that has been, from one April to another, nothing more than a series of variations of winter under twelve different names.

When prophecy is silent in the country you may reckon that things are serious; it is a situation only a little less remarkable than a state – so far unknown – in which gossip is dead. But this year the prophets have not only given up the business of prophecy; they have given up the business of reminiscence. The year, in its cold and torrential gloom, does not remind them of anything. Experience has stored up no memory quite like it. Indefatigable as they are in recalling years that were colder or stormier or wetter or hotter than any you care to name, the country oracles can find no sort of yard stick to measure this one.

What perplexes them too is not merely its peculiarity; it is the continuance of the same stormy, cold, restless and rainy state of things that troubles them. 'I reckon it's alla time a-lettin' orf these ere atom bombs,' a small bright-eyed Kentish man says to me, pert with conviction and triumph as a hen laying an egg, 'or else these ere jets. Never had no good weather since they started 'em. Dammit, it stands to reason they churn up th' atmosphere. Can't be the same as it would if they never churned it up. Needn't wonder the weather gets terrifoid.' Not one single sentence of this theory, propounded in all seriousness, with conviction, and as something freshly unearthed and startling, is new. I first heard it, just as sagely and convincingly propounded, just as serious and triumphant, when I came to live in Kent twenty years ago, and I have no doubt it was here, just as stubborn and triumphant, the day the first balloon went up and the day, a considerable number of centuries past, when gunpowder first blew ball-shot from the barrel of a gun.

I do not want to give the impression that, because of a certain tendency to be more stubborn, more stupid and more plain downright awkward in matters of change than most people, the native of Kent is more horse-headed than other Englishmen. But there is no shadow of doubt that he is an odd, complex, perplexing and in many ways forbidding creature. The peculiar geography of his native country has something, possibly a great deal, to do with this. On the south its sea-coast faces France, from which, over the centuries, came the traditional invaders; on the east the coast faces Flanders, Germany and all Eastern Europe, with possibly a longer tradition of invaders past and still to come; and to the north lies London, from which a conceivably worse sort of invasion, that of other Englishmen if you please, has been going on in one form or another, from hop-pickers to business-men in bowler hats, for centuries. Only one

53

other English county, Cornwall, has a comparable geographical shape, and there it is a commonplace to hear strangers referred to as Englishmen, as opposed to Cornish-men, and to hear of fanatical ladies who desire to separate the county from the main body of the nation, with exalted notions of separate kingship and autonomy.

Englishmen brought up in less isolated, more neighbourly, parts of the country may feel a natural inclination to laugh at these things; but it would never surprise me very much, if at all, to hear that a type of Kentish fanatic, expressing the small-nation nation-alism that is now besetting every scrap of God's earth where more than three people speak a language different from that of their fellows, had bred some sort of society for Kentish self-government. This would not only be in perfect keeping with the con-temporary urge to split up the world into smaller and more aggressively anti-pathetic divisions, rather than to unify it; but it would also be in perfect accord with the notion of Kentish character as it has been my experience to know it – a character almost uniformly isolationary, stubbornly suspicious and resentful to outsiders, impervious in a remarkable way to outside influences, and in a general way saturnine, unsympathetic and difficult to know. It is rare indeed to make friendships in Kent: except, that is, with Yorkshiremen, Scotsmen, Irishmen, men of the Midlands or Lancashire or Somerset, or indeed with people from any other part of the Kingdom. The native of Kent does not give himself easily, if he gives himself at all.

The country of white clover which forms the title to this book is, of course, the country of Kent: and one of the reasons for beginning this book with a description of a spring journey through France was that I have long felt that the two countries were more alike than we sometimes suppose. I have long been tempted by the notion also, and have now accepted it, that the native of Kent and the native of those parts of France bordering the Channel, from Normandy to the Pas de Calais, are near enough the same kind of people.

A market day in Kent is as good a way as any of looking at the odd assortment of vagabondage that scrapes itself up from the land, the villages and the tawdry bungalow settlements of woodsides in order to come into town. The people of Kent are notoriously shabby in dress but on market days, and again on Saturday afternoons, the most astonishing scarecrows come out of their holes. No Midland or Northern town, where smartness among factory girls is as natural as breathing, could tolerate for a moment the rats-tailed blondes, the cutthroat dealers, the sloppy baggy-breasted Amazons street-crawling with smear-nosed children, the lank-haired, side-whiskered youths with back-glancing eyes like crafty hares, or the general air of unwashed scumdom that fills Kentish streets on market day. Maupassant, who knew so well the swindling, prospering, rat-brained peasants of his native Normandy, could have been equally at home here among their dark, bright-cheeked English counterparts. Except in language he could have noted no difference at all. These are the people whose dealings are strictly cash; who distrust banks and all their dealings; whose tongues are as smooth as butter in the art of saying nothing in as many words as possible. Craftiness is not learned here; it is inherent in the southern temperament, luckily born into a rich and bountiful countryside on which it can wax fat.

It is twenty years, almost to the month, since I came to live in Kent, and its special sort of backwardness, which amused me then, surprises me still. It is not merely that here, in a prosperous county close to London, it is common to meet children and grown men who cannot write their names. It is rather the sort of backwardness that is, through pure instinct, holding something back. The Kentish temperament by nature does not tend to give; it withholds. It is possible to know a Kentish man for a quarter of a century and yet not know him at all; you may live next door to him for a generation and he will never invite you over his threshold. All this, perhaps, is the working of his natural distrust of foreigners. But when it comes to receiving something from you, outsider though you are, he exhibits no such scruples. Foreigners, to whom nothing must be given, are fair game when it comes to the art of taking away. As a result the Kentish man has brought to a fine art the business of making anything or everything he does for you a favour. His peasantlike mind, to which all life is instinctively a bargain, does not regard the simple exchange of labour and money as a fair deal in which each side is getting what he needs and what the other has to offer. He is granting, instead, a concession. He is granting it, that is, if he thinks he will. I have known men from London and from other, more open-hearted parts of the Kingdom, filled with impotent despair at this intractable manifestation of pure cussedness, or 'orkardness' as it appears in Kent's own language. I have known sharp London dealers, confronted with this special brand of obstinacy, give up in despair.

To the surface of this interesting and maddening temperament there is very often attached, it must be admitted, an immense politeness. A good deal of cap-touching survives. Young men who canter about the primrose lanes, exercising horses, put their fingers to the peaks of their caps and call you sir. A church-warden, hurrying to morning services, raises his hat. In the bar of the pub there is a respectful hush as you enter and a rapid downing of half-drunk pints before your hand is on your money. A bantering warmth is to be bought, then, for a shilling or two. If you are a newcomer, fresh to this wonderful county of cherry-orchards and miles of sweet chestnut and white clover and flourishing corn and apple-blossom, all unexcelled in England, then you may fall for a time into the deception that here, in surroundings of great loveliness, is a droll, generous, lively people.

On the very first evening I came into Kent, more than twenty years ago, on a dark February night, I was struck by the intricate pattern of its deep lanes and, in one place by the flashing length of a piece of oak fencing, half a mile or more long, about a park.

Today, after a quarter of a life-time, the fence and the park, or at least thirty-five acres of it, belong to me. Spread out on a series of slopes and indentations that give it something of the appearance of a huge round and battered hat, this piece of land was once part of the domain of a great house. You can see quite easily that its present character, its shape and the design of its trees, dates from the time when the creation of parklands out of simple agricultural land was the popular craze of English country gentlemen. The squares and oblongs of lost fields are still there, as clear as the undulations marking the earthworks of an early settlement. A mile away, on a high point, the great house, reputedly lived in by a single family far longer than any house in England, stares down.

In 1929, in the great slump, disaster fell. In a series of sales, that summer, farms and woodlands, cottages and orchards, the park and the great house itself, were split and sold. The familiar, modern destructive pattern spread out. Timber merchants arrived and, locust-like, swarmed on the vast eighteenth century design of oaks and beeches and sweet-chestnuts. An area of land that had been almost black in summer with the heavy draperies of trees in their prime was suddenly transformed into something resembling one of those scarred battle-fields of Flanders out of the war of which the slump was only a bloodless continuation. Only the sagacity of the original planter of trees, whose memory I bless, saved a hundred or so trees from destruction. This wiseacre of the eighteenth century, loving trees and looking two centuries ahead, had had the intelligent thought to plant about half his park with useless timber. Thus the turkey-oaks, the hornbeams, the horse-chestnut, many of the beeches and most of the sweet-chestnuts were saved.

The rest were felled with the pointless and wanton abandon of an invading army. Trunks were tossed about the slopes of grass and left where they lay. Soon, and not surprisingly in an era of bankruptcy, a timber merchant here went out of business and another forgot the timber lying on a Kentish hill. Already, two years later, when I first knew it, time and nature were well at work. A group of twenty-five sweet-chestnuts, tall as steeples, exposed by the felling of surrounding trees, had been bitterly withered by the terrible winter of 1929, so that their tender tops were now nothing but skeleton belfries for flocks of roosting starlings. Felled beeches, soft with fungus, were crumbling to orange pulp in the grass.

Brambles were smothering dead stumps. A few beeches, exposed to wind by ruthless felling, had fallen naturally, yellow roots sticking up from watery craters. The fence, beautifully made of patterned cleft oak – an art now as dead as the painting of primitive pictures in caves – was falling down. Nettles were spreading everywhere under the remaining trees and rabbits were settling down, in their ugly fashion, into vast warrens on the slopes of grass.

A second war for freedom had not then taught the English the high value of the land on which they live and slowly, inevitably, desolately, thirty-five acres of land began to decay into useless dereliction, into fungoid weedy ugliness, the grave of a man of taste and ambition who had walked about it, no doubt with joy, two hundred years before. I wonder continually what sort of man he was. The planting of young trees, always a joyful thing, is nevertheless tempered by a cooling sadness: by the thought that, unless you plant them as a child and live for nearly a century, you will never see them in their fullest, ripest beauty. The new young trunks, with spindly arms and little ears of leaves, are so fragile; they look so lifeless and useless and will never grow up. Impatiently one wants to see them cast enough shade to comfort at least a dog. The thought that lovers two centuries hence will be lying on a hot June day under the oak that now looks like a broomstick is one that needs a brave heart to contemplate with joy. Small wonder that we plant trees that ramp into maturity.

But here was a man who planted, nearly everywhere, trees of slow and sturdy growth. No birches and poplars and willows for him, but beeches and turkey-oaks that needed a century, perhaps two, to spread themselves. His selfishness could only have been in direct proportion to his courage, and his courage, I hope, to his happiness at the thought that in succeeding years whole generations of Englishmen would be able to extract the greatest joy from the things he had done. But Time, two centuries later, put up a dirty finger at him; and by 1940, when an anti-aircraft battery stood camouflaged under the decaying bony chestnuts, his picture had nearly finished its long slide into decay.

It went on, in that way, for another seven or eight years. I watched it most of the time. War gave a long holiday to nettles and brambles, thistles and rabbits, docks and briars. Bright orange fungus, together with long blue-grey veins of delicate netting, the spores of a decay as beautiful as the veil of a woman's hat, ate a crumbling pulpy way over fallen beech trunks. More trees fell down. The fences became hidden in vast prickly cushions of bramble, purple and white in early summer, black with fruit in August and September, and gradually under the weight of them, the fences fell down. Hurdles began to be used to fill up the gaps and then they too, under a weight of briar and blackberry and ivy, collapsed. On the south boundary were two little ponds, on one of which moorhens nested in clumps of sedge among white-eyed ferns of water ranunculus. Gradually more trees fell into the ponds. Then hot summers dried the ponds, revealing desolate basins of brown cracked mud littered with tin cans. In efforts to prevent the fences falling down still further someone strung them together with lengths of barbed wire, and someone else linked two trees together with a thin wire hawser in the hope, evidently, that that too would prevent a fall. Somehow barbed wire, and then more wire, and then scraps of sheet netting, began to be littered about the grass. The two gates fell down. A great arm of the most magnificent of all the beeches split off in a gale, and in the fissure caused in the trunk a blackberry took root and helped in the process of eating it away. The soil, impoverished, thinning like a balding head, under the poison of rabbits, gave every autumn its crop of elegant brown-spotted fungus, gilled and hooded like things from a fairy tale, and then hosts of thin papery leaves came down from the chestnut-trees and drifted dryly against the fences, until spring winds blew them away. Above it all the tall dead skeletons of the chestnut-trees, ugly and infinitely desolate, stood like stag-horns, to be seen for miles and miles about the countryside, gaunt trophies marking, as it were, the death of a great herd.

There had been indeed, almost up to that time, a herd of deer that roamed, eight hundred strong, about the park and the woodlands beside it, and it was a lovely sight – almost the only sight of anything like loveliness left to the place – to see the running ghost-like creatures, tense and dapple-trembling and shy, disappearing into the shadow of distant beeches from open land. But war came and among its unrecorded casualties are the eight hundred deer, wiped out by bored and mischievous soldiers having hunting parties with service rifles and .303. When the deer had gone the rabbits remained in possession, together with shrilly explosive flocks of starlings and an occasional fox, so old that it was almost the tawny-yellow colour of a pale barnyard hen, roaming with casual arrogance, in broad daylight, from one farm to another.

Not less amazing than this long unchecked decay were the reasons that caused it. The park, or that seventeen acres of it that I was to buy first, had belonged, astonishing though it may seem, to a lady who loved trees. Into her head had at some time penetrated the notion, never afterwards to be removed, that trees were untouchable things. In health, in decay, in age, in the air or on the ground, they were to be left, evidently, as God shaped them. It may well be thought that such curiously inverted affection is, even among old ladies, something unique. I do not think so. The English countryside is heavily populated with an infinite number of old ladies, living alone or in pairs, whose lives are just such engaging contradictions of ugliness and love. Surrounded by hordes of cats, by hosts of tea-drinking dogs, by goats whose uselessness is only equalled by their incomparable astringent goat-like odour, they drape their fading lives about strange houses, in strange ways, and are an eternal and incontestable part of our sometimes queer and inexplicable rural background.

So if a piece of England slipped far down into ugly decay because love, even in the simplest way, was not practical, it was by no means unique. All around the same thing was happening. It is not to be expected that trees are eternal and it was not surprising that, after two hundred years, beeches and even chestnuts were beginning to fall like tired soldiers. For all this the old ladies had no remedy but a desperate wringing of hands. A timber merchant even tells the story of how, seeing a great and magnificent beech crashed across the lawn at a house, he called on its owner, an old lady of eighty, to suggest its speedy clearance, with some payment in consolation for its timber. Angrily, and with tears, as at the death of a relation on which he had wantonly intruded, he was driven from the house.

It sometimes seems to me that men of earlier centuries had a swifter and more effective way of dealing with the infuriating female tyrants that are the everlasting pest and persecution of every village. They simply called them witches. Eccentricity, gossip, nosiness, back-biting and plain female cattiness could be endured for just so long and no longer. If nature could not act, men could. A ducking stool or a few faggots at the stake did the rest.

Nowadays they live longer; but in time even old ladies, like trees, drop down. So it happened at last that the first acres of parkland came into the market. Utterly inexperienced in the art of pretending we did not want something when in fact we wanted it with all our hearts we rushed to the estate agent, only to be told that old familiar, artful story:

'Ah! yes, we have already had several *firm* offers for this property. Of course we don't know what *figure* you had in mind. And of course we have no wish to conduct a *private* auction.'

We had a modest, reasonable, fair and decent figure in mind. We mentioned it. It was as if we had offered fifty shillings or so for an option on the crown jewels. We were treated to a smile of tired and tolerant scorn.

'Well, of course, we could *submit* it to our client. We can only *submit* it. But as I say – there have been other offers.'

Sickly we went away; we made calculations and consulted; and in due course the telephone rang:

'I feel it only fair to tell you that our client has received an offer of fifty pounds *above* your own. Of course we have no wish to conduct a *private* auction. We don't like that sort of thing. But there you *are*.'

There indeed we were. Never in my life had I owned more than an acre of land. Here, neglected and derelict, it was true, but wide and free and potentially beautiful, were seventeen. They lay in the heart of the country I thought to be the most beautiful in England; from them, on fine clear days, you could see, far away, southward, the line of Sussex coast and the rim of sea. I wanted them badly: with intolerable, stupid, possessive, maddeningly, childish longing. And why, I would ask myself, why not? There were men about me who owned acres of England in thousands; they could not count their legions of trees; they could lose themselves in hillsides of vast deep woodland. Beside them the possession of seventeen bramble-ridden, fungus-rotted acres seemed a joke. For years, as the land slipped down into ugly decay, it seemed less and less as if anyone could conceivably wish to own it. Now, if we were to believe suave dry voices on the telephone, a dozen people wished to do so. They clamoured for it. And suddenly, stubbornly, stupidly and pig-headedly I determined they should clamour in vain.

Angrily I tossed the rules of the game overboard and, in one prodigiously reckless moment, shot up the price by a hundred pounds. There were a few moments of, I thought, a sort of deflated disappointment: as if it were not quite in order, not quite done, to indulge in such recklessness at a moment when the game was about to settle down. It was like a too-easy checkmate at chess. In one too swiftly painful move the thing was over.

So I became, in the most modest sort of way, and after all really not too expensively, a landowner. In forty-eight hours gossip, always so clairvoyant and vigilant, credited me with the intention of building a mansion, a bungalow, six bungalows, a row of cottages, and of becoming a farmer.

Airily, freely and without rancour, I let it be known that every single part of it was true.

It was now April: cold and dry and unfriendly, without a leaf of green on the trees. Winter drought and hard spring wind had dried old grass into yellow tussocks tangled with drifting dead chestnut-leaves. With the wind blowing easterly, away from the road, we set fire to the grass, letting it burn where it would. The fires rambled in blue and orange drifts, leaving black patterns, and while they burned we contemplated our assets, living and dead, on this piece of England.

We had, it seemed, something like this: twenty-five standing sweet-chestnuts, very tall, all dead at the tips; eight standing beeches, of which one was a shaky and magnificent ruin, six dead beeches and one fallen; three hornbeams and two ash-trees and two elms, each gigantic and wonderful; six turkey-oaks, all sound and three superb, and two maples, one shapely and delightful; an unspecified number of elder bushes and hawthorns, all old, crabbed and witch-like, and a still greater number of blackberries, briars and seedling ashes. Of the dead beeches some stood like skeletons, some were crumbling fallen masts of orange and black and purple fungus. There were two ponds, half-filled with the junk of war-time, two broken gates and about a mile of derelict fencing. Of living creatures we had, as far as I could judge, a pair of grey wagtails, whose prinkings and dancings on the April grass were like the pert machinations of little toys, a storm-thrush, a rookery of about twenty nests in the big beeches, a covey of thirteen partridges, an uncountable number of grey squirrels, an owl and a prodigious stinking stoat that was later killed by a dog. There were also rabbits. How many of them I never knew, but paradise had gone on for them a long, long time. There were also dog violets, primroses and, among the fifty or so dead tree-stumps where the rabbits played, a few blue-bells.

We brought fire, hawsers, tractors, and trucks to the dead trees, which went up on a fine windy April evening in a hell-fire exploding bonfire. During the days of its later burning I called in my friend the timber merchant and, on a dry and withering afternoon, overcoated against the first blasts of spring, we went to inspect the chestnut-trees whose gaunt antlers, on that high point, were so much a landmark and an eyesore.

'You want them down?' the timber merchant said and then began to explain, in the polite, brisk and devastating manner of experts, that Spanish chestnut is, as timber, about as valuable as old rope. 'That of course,' he explained for my benefit, 'is why that original artful old devil planted them.'

But I did not, I explained, want them down. 'I want them topped,' I said. 'Preserved.'

'*Topped?*' My friend the timber merchant, who is a kindly, friendly gentle sort of man, drew into his overcoat with horror. '*Preserved?*'

'Topped,' I said.

'Up *there?*'

'Up there,' I said.

We paced about. An April tree, naked, sixty or seventy feet high, seems, as you stand directly underneath it and look up to its tip, at least a hundred and fifty feet high; and as we stood there looking up a perfectly genuine and awful horror broke out in my friend.

'But it can't be *done*. It isn't *possible*. Up *there?*' He began to mutter shakenly about fire escapes. He tried to console me by saying that of course to *fell* the trees – that was his pigeon, that was a different matter. 'But getting up *there!* There's no ladder long enough. I haven't a man who would risk it. It is a thousand to one we'd have someone killed.'

Horrified, he let me lead him dismally away.

It was here, or very shortly afterwards, that I heard of Mr Kimmins. Spring now began to warm slowly into what was to be an exquisite summer and on a golden day of oak-flowers and may-blossom, with tender hand-dappling wind, Mr Kimmins, a reticent, gentle spoken Cockney of about fifty-five or sixty, came down from his native

Wandsworth, filled with life-long affection for and ripe knowledge of trees.

Mr Kimmins and I had a cup of tea together and then I took him to the park. Mr Kimmins, patient and possessed, looked up at the impossible chestnuts. I, in fear, looked at Mr Kimmins.

Mr Kimmins, continuing to look at the chestnuts, which were just leafing in the spring sun, did not speak. I, anxiously, began to say once again how I should like them topped; I explained that I knew how very high they were and how very difficult it all was. There had, I thought, been quite enough trees destroyed in England, and in Kent especially, of late years, and it seemed to me quite time that a few were preserved. Cuckoos called in the quiet air while Mr Kimmins cogitated these matters. I did not know whether Mr Kimmins was friend or enemy, acrobat or just another timber merchant, and Mr Kimmins, wandering to and fro under the high trees with myself following him like an obedient dog, gave no sign to enlighten me.

It is notable that all your pet ideas, which in the homely warmth of your own brain seem so beautifully fresh, original and practical, seem at once appallingly clumsy and stupid and impossible as soon as you bring them out for appraisal in the cold air of expert opinion. This is especially true in matters of gardening, carpentry, building and architecture and had been so, as far as my experience went, in arboriculture. No timber man I had ever met knew anything more about trees than that they ought, as soon as possible, to be cut down. I am in fact convinced that the cutting down of trees, like the process of hacking treasured shrubs to the ground, is an enormously popular one. Nothing delights a certain type of male mind – women are entirely excluded from these remarks – than the possession of saws, axes, ropes and a good sound healthy tree in an awkward place. A few years ago my own village was presented with a plantation of about a hundred trees, including some exceptionally beautiful things such as acacias, African oaks, planes and limes, all of ripe and sound maturity. Possession had hardly been taken of this delightful oval of woodland, all the more precious because it stood in the middle of the village street, than the tree-chopping minds rose up to take their harvest. In two fierce days chaotic and irretrievable ruin was wrought on everything that bore leaf or twig. No reason, either economic or aesthetic, practical or otherwise, was ever advanced for this block-headed behaviour; no comment ever offered except the un-failing one from those thick-heads who, in all villages, delight in the art of standing well back from whatever of importance is going on in order to be able to laugh, jeer or belch louder when the time comes:

'Ah! yis, but it wun arf let some dayloight in.'

From the time of that splendidly en-lightened remark until the moment I stood under the chestnut trees with Mr Kimmins an unconscionable and increasing amount of daylight had been let in not only in my own village but all over England. Daylight was something we were not short of; trees, everywhere, were the price we were paying for it. The long and beautiful inheritance of English trees was being squandered, if that is not too harsh a word, by the two essentially destructive games at which modern man is so adept: War and taxation. Through them, by painful labour, we were now well on the road to the evolution of a type that had free false teeth but nothing to eat with them, supersonic planes but no fire on his hearth and who might well end up, as a cabinet minister so aptly pointed out, sitting by a television set, starving.

I do not go quite so far as this; but it has long seemed to be an arguable proposition that if we go on translating trees into taxes and taxes into teeth, or into wooden legs or wooden heads or whatever it may be, we may well devise for ourselves a state in which man is state-protected, in sickness and in health, from the cradle to the grave, and will be forced at the same time to spend his days staring at a treeless landscape of petrol pumps and pylons. Impossible to deny that this is a fanciful exaggeration; impossible to deny, also, that in the last ten years England has lost, at the most random estimate, some millions of her trees.

So as I stood with Mr Kimmins in the park my anxiety was that not a tree of my own should, if possible be cut down.

'I know how difficult it is,' I said to Mr Kimmins again. 'I know they say people might get killed. But if–'

'*Killed?*' Mr Kimmins said. '*Difficult? That? – up there?*'

'Yes, but isn't it?...'

'Good gracious me,' Mr Kimmins said, 'we come from London. We're doing it every day. *Difficult?* In London we have to take down trees a yard at a time – bit by bit, every bit slung on a pulley. *Difficult?*' Mr Kimmins laughed. 'Bless me, I fink this a nice straight-forward little job.'

'You mean it can be *done?*'

'Yus,' Mr Kimmins said. 'It can be done.'

It now seemed to me that Mr Kimmins was filled with sudden warmth and affection for the trees. Walking about, pointing, explaining, he became enthusiastically eloquent.

'Now I tell you what we'll do. We'll have 'em all orf darn to the green wood. Yus: that's what we'll do. Have 'em orf nice an' clean darn to the green wood. Then they'll make new heads, see? In two-free years you won't know they bin cut orf.' Now and then Mr Kimmins paused to lay a large, friendly, expert hand on that peculiarly twisted pleasant bark that is characteristic of the Spanish chestnut in maturity. 'Very nice trees they are. Very nice. Be a fahrsand pities to let 'em go.'

'I said so all along.'

'I fink so,' Mr Kimmins said. 'I fink it'd be a fahrsand pities.' Mr Kimmins paused before a tree that, in the rough sad years of neglect, had been blasted to a crackled gnarled ruin of a giant. 'Now there's a tree there. Take 'im. He's wurf saving. He don't look much. But we'll have a limb orf there an' another limb orf there and another bit orf of 'is top an' in a couple o' years you won't know 'im.'

Mr Kimmins, genial, friendly and infinitely intelligent, warmed my heart. Steadily, with care and affection, we diagnosed the troubles and needs of sixty trees. The chestnuts needed deep surgical operations at the tops; here and there a beech, far gone with fungus, would have to come down; there would be a few loppings of ash and elm. We even attended to a stag-headed maple and an ancient hawthorn. Trees I had considered hopeless, too far gone with split and water-rotten trunks, were put down in Mr Kimmins' casebook as patients that could still be saved.

There were three such beeches. It is characteristic of the beech, so magnificent everywhere in this part of Kent, that its fat smooth trunk allows the passage of rain water down into the deep armpits of the limbs: so that gradually, in time, the central trunk is eaten away. Beeches in full prime and beauty suddenly split and fall, simply destroyed by the long slow seepage of rain. The remedy is simple. A shelf of concrete, sloped to allow water to pitch from the trunk instead of into it, will keep a beech dry and healthy during the difficult years when its own girth and weight, collecting rain, are the worst enemies to its survival. We doctored, in that way, a beech that had already lost a heavy limb, tearing away in its fall nearly half the central trunk, leaving a funnel that collected rain. It survives today, beautiful and healed and healthy.

But before I said goodbye to Mr Kimmins in that first interview there was something else I wanted to ask him. I was still troubled by the chestnuts; I wanted to know exactly how that lofty surgical operation, sixty or seventy feet from the ground, was done: whether there would be fire-escapes or cradles or pulleys or steam saws, or what peculiar paraphernalia and devices these experts from the city, faced with country projects, would employ.

'How do you get up there?' I said.

'We climbs up,' Mr Kimmins said.

'Yes, but what with?'

'Ladders.'

'What sort of ladders? Special ones? Fire-escapes?'

'Just ladders.'

'And then the sawing part,' I said. 'How is that done?'

'Wiv saws.'

'Yes: but what sort of saws?'

'Ordinary saws.'

'Cross-cut?'

'Panel,' Mr Kimmins said.

Humbled and silenced, I gave up. Later I was to be further humbled; but that day, as I said goodbye to the modest, friendly, tree-loving and knowledgeable Mr Kimmins, I was reminded of the truth that not all countrymen live in the country. And the thought of Mr Kimmins, Cockney born and

Cockney to the heart, about to perform a countryman's job in a way countrymen had thought impossible, was something that gave me a special kind of pleasure.

'When will you start?' I said.

'In a fortnight or free weeks,' Mr Kimmins said. 'The wevver should be nice by then.'

4 Trees and Man

The weather was indeed nice; late spring came into fullness with golden days of oak-flower and buttercup, of grass deepening to lush and fragrant seed. On the park's impoverished soil a crop of pinky-copper sorrel flowered, waving on days of wind and sun like stained water. Moorhens laid eggs for the seventh or eighth time, in their domestically persistent way, on the small ponds, and the sweet-chestnuts broke into almost yellow leaf that only heightened, more now than ever, the grey gauntness of their dead tops.

Duly, in a red truck piled with ladders, ropes, saws and suitcases, Mr Kimmins and his men arrived. There were four of them, and they looked rather like the committee of a Working Men's Club out for a day in the country. Neatly efficient, cheerful and in some curious way taut and confident, they lacked all rural gaucheness of bearing and attitude. Beside the surrounding countrymen, slack and slovenly and with that plummy rolling gait that work on the land so often gives, they had a look of being really emancipated, of politely and simply not caring a damn.

This, as it turned out, proved to be entirely correct. Time, in the sense of clocking in at a doorway at eight in the morning and clocking out at five in the evening, did not exist for them. They were, in the best sense, manual artists, and as artists they worked: not to time or to rule, with eyes on the clock or the time-table, but entirely according to the physical demand of the job. On Mondays they did not appear much before lunchtime and on Fridays they left by early afternoon; it was a short week, but within its limits they performed what I thought were exceptionally interesting wonders.

The essence of a first-class woodman

engaged in the business of high tree-lopping is that he shall be able to climb. It is essential also that he should begin young. Once he learns to climb, acquiring something of the poise and confidence of a steeplejack at the same time, his arts consists to a great degree in what he learns about trees. They have peculiarities which can kill him if he is a fool. Much of what he has to do with trees is concerned with weight, and intelligent assessment of weight has everything to do with a job that afterwards, in good hands, seems simpler than pruning a rose.

Sam, Mr Kimmins' foreman, a smallish, compact, dark-haired Londoner, was a man who had learned to climb, expertly as a boy, and had been climbing ever since. His methods looked peculiarly simple, almost amateurish and off hand. His procedure was simply to climb halfway up the tree by ladder, and then up to the top of the tree, exactly like a boy birds' nesting, by hand. He took a rope with him. This rope was presently lowered so that his saw, an ordinary carpenter's panel saw, could be sent up to him. It was lowered again for a second rope and this second rope was tied to the top of the tree.

All this looked so ridiculously simple that it was some days before I noticed a highly important thing. Sam, who climbed the tree in two minutes, often spent nearly an hour looking at it. Walking round and round it, assessing and cogitating, he went into the problems of weight with the expert's care. Only when he was satisfied with that would he begin to climb.

Thereafter, as Mr Kimmins had so rightly seemed to declare, the thing was child's play. Sam, alone and unhurried, sat in the tree and sawed. He sawed for perhaps twenty minutes: first through the tree-trunk one way and then for twenty minutes, according to the size of the tree, the other. When the trunk hung by no more than a couple of inches of its centre Sam sat back, directed his mates down below on the end of the rope and gave the order to pull. The tree top, partly carried by distribution of weight, described a long and graceful arc that took it quite clear of both tree and Sam, and the whole thing with a bouncing crash of bony timber, was suddenly all over.

In that way Sam dealt with about twenty sweet-chestnuts and three turkey-oaks, two of which were eighty feet high, and only twice, when extra poundage was needed on the end of the rope, did he trouble to come down to earth when the tree-top was felled. Small, confident, calmer than any bird, he sat half-hidden by rapidly leafing branches and watched each tree shed its gaunt antlers in safety.

No local countryman had ever seen such amazing curious acts in trees and the whole procedure remained, for three weeks, a spring-time wonder. In their true slow Kentish fashion, intensely cautious, partly dubious, half-suspicious, filled with con- sistent unadventurousness, they sat back to marvel greatly. This marvelling included me. Writers of books being in any case not quite of the sanity of other people it was, perhaps, not altogether surprising that I was trying to preserve trees instead of cutting them down and chopping them up, as any sensible person would, for firewood. But to have trees lopped, at the tops, by men from London and no doubt at great expense, was something hard to understand. To this patient proof of the natural insanity of writers was added, as always, with unfailing consistency, the wails of the ever-present old ladies for whom, in the country, it is so difficult ever to do the right thing. 'Oh! but we shall *miss* the old tops. We *loved* them, they'd been there so *long*. They were such a landmark.'

May flowed warmly into June. Large and thick and shining, the leaves of the sweet-chestnuts unfurled to full pattern, hiding the pruned tree-tops, so that the trees, in their new neatness, were pyramids of brilliant green. Vast piles of cordwood had accumulated. Two trunks, one of which had lain for twenty years or more in beds of bramble and nettle, had been sent off to the saw-mill and now came back in the form of an almost orange-coloured, still sappy timber. Wreck and ruin were everywhere being cleared away; the splendidly beautiful shape of the remaining beeches, deprived now of dead boughs and general muck, was fully revealed, and to me at any rate no trees had ever looked more lovely or more worth possessing. Mr Kimmins and Sam did a last round up, stopping holes, painting cut limbs, cementing gullies and, in Sam's case, catching a last rabbit for the missus among the brambles. Mr Kimmins, sound and knowledgeable and pleasant as ever, declared once again, perhaps for the fortieth time, that in 'two-free years you won't see where them tops is bin cut' and today, three years afterwards, his words of modest prophecy are coming true.

We acquired, about this time, quite by accident, in a casual way, the services of another admirable character, no less pleasant and sound than Mr Kimmins and the wonderfully efficient Sam. He came to us originally for the simple purpose of putting up a gate: a man of medium height and age, roundish and yet in some way square, pleasant, droll, cryptic, slow and given to occasional bursts of bright invective, all the more devastating because they were, generally, monosyllabic, Saxon and exceedingly short. William was a carpenter utterly removed from the rest of his tribe by the fact that he never grizzled, never blamed the tools or the absence of them, never criticized any of the timber, in this case mostly the despised chestnut, we had to offer. Soundly, complaintlessly, in his own time and way, William set about the business of repairing what was to prove, eventually, about a mile of cleft fencing. In days when cleaving and cleavers were as much a part of rural economy as cowmen and horsekeepers it was common practice for cleavers to arrive at farms, inquire for work and then settle down to cleave out, mostly from oak, enough fence paling for a farmer's needs. This cleft fencing is not only amazingly durable but, in its fanciful and unsquared shapes, winged and pinned and tailed, extremely beautiful. Age gives it a cheese-like greenness softly powdered with grey silver. Only accident and neglect, of which ours had suffered much, seem capable of destroying it, and even then its powers of endurance and survival are a wonder. Some long and hopeless sections of our broken-down fencing had been so long hidden by brambles that we had given them up completely as irreparable and lost. Here and there sections were flat on the ground. Posts were, or appeared to be, quite rotten. But the durability of oak and especially of cleft oak was such that when we set about the business of removing whole sections for replacement we found it completely un-necessary, a situation summed up with grim and final brevity by William who said:

'Lumme, if them soddin' posts ain't arf in there.'

William continued to come to us from then onwards with what I can best describe as consistent irregularity. Time, hours, instructions, orders were things that did not come between us. He came, went and worked in his own peculiar time and way. Timber and fence being there, close together, it was only necessary to marry them, restoring order and decency: a task for which William was admirably gifted, with his unhurried skill and temperament, without interference from me. Only now and then would he deliver to me, in cryptic and crushing terms, a lecture on the necessity of remembering that, after all, material things do sometimes matter:

'If you want your bloody fence mendin' you better git them nails.'

'I know. I'm sorry – I forgot.'

'You keep on forgittin'. You goo orf to bloody London and you forgit.'

'I've been terribly busy.'

'Well, you doant wanna be so busy. You wanna remember them nails.'

'All right. I'll get them tomorrow. Now what sizes and how many?'

'I writ it all down for you on a bit o' paper and now you bin orf to bloody London again and forgot it, ainyer?'

'I'm afraid so.'

'God 'eads like bloody sieves, some people.'

All this, profoundly true as it was, I could not deny. It was delivered also with a drollery, a sort of dry richness, not without a certain sadness, that was quite without offence. And how true it was, in a sense, that gooin' orf to bloody London was not to be compared with the sensible and necessary business of getting the nails without which even the most good-natured and accommodating carpenters cannot work. I will not deny, either, that there were occasions when I forgot on purpose, solely for the pleasure of hearing that droll, withering, yet tolerant voice tell me:

'If you don' want that bloody timber o' yourn to goo rot and warp all over the soddin' place you better let me git it seen to and turned over.'

'All right: you see to it.'

'You'll ev it bloody warp if you don't. It's bloody warpin' now.'

'When you like. Carry on.'

'Lumme, if it ain' arf 'ot up there too.'

Thirst being an essential part of the carpentry trade this hint would not be lost on me. Some time later, bearing a bottle or two of beer up to the deep shade of the turkey-oaks, than which in summer there is nothing cooler or blacker, I would find William moving piles of timber with that unhurried and unvaried pace that takes the countryman through his sixteen hour summer day.

'And I bet you ain't got them bloody nails, 'ave yer?'

'Tomorrow, for sure. Tomorrow–'

'Don't matter! I got some o' me own now. If I wait for you, I'll wait till the bloody cows come 'ome.'

So, through the long, hot, almost unblemished summer, William helped to restore final decency and material soundness to the park. Not the least of his many virtues was adaptability. He made us, in our modest way, self-supporting. We spoke, on one occasion, of buying gates.

'Gates? *Buying* gates? You got the damn timber here, ainyer? What th' 'ell's the damn timber for? Buy gates?– Good God!'

A good part of my life having been spent in apologizing to workmen, both young and old, for the primitive nature of the materials I have to offer them, I had hardly dared to suggest to William that he should make gates.

'You jis tell me what sorta gate you want and I'll git it made for you. Drop gate? 'Anging gate? Then I can git the furniture made at the forge.'

So William, repairing fences to their old lost pattern, a pattern that will never be seen again, making gates for us in a few hours on a Sunday morning, turning his hand to any job we cared to name or that he liked to suggest that we, in our appalling London-wise ignorance, had forgotten, became for us, and indeed still remains, a sterling example of what we think a countryman should be and so rarely is. He seems to us a character, from the bone of his blue-eyed head down to his efficient adaptable hands, purely and wonderfully English. Dry, forthright, droll, decent, warm, immensely resourceful, respectful but never servile, he belongs, in spite of an ability to drive a tractor about the countryside like any modern mechanized god, to any century of our rural history. To call him complaintless is not quite correct. Once, and once only, I heard him complain with cryptic forth-rightness, offering his brief comment on our strange world of false teeth, low diet, high politics and theoretical securities, the world of whose future pattern we have already had a glimpse in the picture of men sitting by their television sets, starving to death, and no doubt illiterate too:

'I don' git enough in my belly. And when I

don't git enough in my belly I carn't bloody work. And when I carn't bloody work it ain' so well.'

5 Union Rustic

Readers of an earlier work of mine, *The Country Heart,* may recall a character named Mr Pimpkins, arch-type of all jobbing gardeners, the horticultural tyrant who subjects your precious shrubs to a process known as 'settin' back,' after which, as he so aptly and truthfully remarks, 'You wun arf see a difference in 'em,' and whose rude and erratic ways impose such a stifling dictatorship on your garden that you eventually wonder, in despair, whether it belongs to you or to him. Mr Pimpkins, I think, will always be with us here in England, but there are also signs that, in his tiresome and bigoted way, especially in the business of settin' back, he is international. I have lately seen a Monsieur Pimpkins at work in France; I know of a Herr Pimpkins, still more unshakably stubborn and of the peasantry even than his French and English counterpart, in Switzerland; and in Madeira, in spring, when a wonderful luxuriance of flower and creeper rises everywhere in superb and prodigal splendour, I saw a bare-footed, sun-bathed Señor Pimpkins, with all the peculiar smugness and glee of his tribe, settin' back a hedge of wistaria, bignonia and rose that was about to reach full flower. Armed with his universal tribal weapon, the shears, Señor Pimpkins was reducing to a dismally shaven and geometrical neatness a hedge that would otherwise have been, and no doubt was, the pride and joy of its owner. But no doubt Señor Pimpkins, enveloped as always in evil clouds of smoke rising from the Portuguese equivalent of shag, had already settled any arguments about that by announcing that 'You wun arf see a difference in it when I've done.'

In the seven ages of gardening, beginning with the high priesthood of alpines and ending with the carpet-slipper era of two fuchsias and a maidenhair fern in pots in a warm south window, the fourth, or perhaps the fifth, is that of I-think-we-can-do-it-just-as-well-ourselves. This stage, reached generally in middle life, at a time when stomach measurements are important, follows inevitably on an era of Mr Pimpkins. For two years your most delicious and important shrubs have been subject to the relentless process of constant settin' back, in consequence of which they have never flowered; the rock garden has been dug two spits deep and heavily manured, as a consequence of which your alpines, 'when they git 'olt on it,' assume the grossness of prize cabbages, if they have not already been mercilessly uprooted and burned, in which case it is not at all unlikely that they will be replaced, when your back is turned, by groups of Paul Crampel geranium, bedding calceolaria and Mr Pimpkins' favourite flower, the blue lobelia, so that the whole has something of the appearance of a suburban cemetery.

During all this time it has been exceedingly difficult for you to get a new potato or a green pea raised for your own consumption before mid-July, largely because Mr Pimpkins 'don't 'old with it, you'll git 'em frorsted,' but also because several hours a day have been spent, in Mr Pimpkins' maddening fashion, in growing your sweet-peas on the cordon system, a practice you abhor, purely because Mr Pimpkins is 'goon ev 'em in the show August Monday.' That stupendously important date in history having come and gone, at a benefit to Mr Pimpkins of twenty-five shillings in prize money and a debt to you of seven or eight pounds in labour, you shortly afterwards commit one of those acts of heresy for which there is no forgiveness and indeed no remedy but cold and final estrangement between the parties. To Mr Pimpkins' credit he has succeeded in growing, with incomparable magnificence, a vegetable with which you yourself have always dismally failed and of which you are very fond, the cauliflower. On a fine September morning you descend on the vegetable garden for the simple purpose of cutting a cauliflower for lunch when you are arrested by a cry, from the potting-shed window, as of sepulchral, ulcerated and mortal pain. It is Mr Pimpkins, foaming at the mouth what seems to be a revolting mixture of bread, cheese and wet mustard. This dribbles down his shirt front: to be followed, when soberer breath can be drawn, by the announcement, delivered between clenched pale teeth, that 'You carnt ev them because I'm goon put 'em in the Workin' Men's fust Sat'day in October.' At this grossly impossible announcement an impotent rage rushes through you, weakening as a purge; Mr Pimpkins, recovering colour, assumes the bridled, outraged appearance of a pop-eyed hen; and together you glare across the cauliflowers, which you yourself now observe are being coddled and sheltered under enormous hats of leaf and baggage like pale choice females that must not see the sun, in mutual, speechless hatred. From that day forward you know that it is simply a question of time before Mr Pimpkins announces, with fierce grievance, but to your own sweet and jubilant relief, that 'I sharn't be coming this way no more.'

The final absence of Mr Pimpkins has immediate and refreshing reactions. The garden is now your own. With a certain rash self-satisfaction you remind yourself that you are, after all, still a young man. Half an hour with the hoe, an hour with the spade, a few minutes with rake or pruning shears: these are things that, not so long ago, you did with enjoyment and ease before breakfast. You casually mention this at supper, when to your astonishment and joy your wife announces that 'now the children are at school I've got absolutely nothing to do and it would be simply marvellous to cut the lawn and do things like that again.' After supper, in a garden unpolluted by Mr

Pimpkins' shag, you throw off bold suggestions by which the two of you, with a little system and self-denial, can keep the garden down and save the money. At this point you recall an important and most pressing appointment in London the following day; but your wife, undismayed, says not to worry, because the one thing she adores is mowing the lawn, especially when it's wet in September, and without her stockings on.

Next day London is hot, steamy and profoundly exhausting. You arrive home by a later train than you would have liked, worn-out but much comforted by the recollection that the lawn will be cool and shorn after the unseasonal heat of the day. But as you enter the garden you observe that the lawn has not been mown. Your wife is not to be seen, and the doors and windows of the greenhouse, which you carelessly forgot to open in the morning, are closed tight, giving a paralysing temperature under the glass of a hundred and ten.

Innumerable pots of begonias, with their tender fleshy leaves, and all the late fuchsias, to which you are most sentimentally attached, stand as if withered by fire. Chaos and attrition have spread among the coleus, which droop like half-rinsed washing. Outside, your pots of chrysanthemum, full of buds and also dear to your heart, are utterly shrivelled and lie drooping on the path. The lawn has grown two inches in the steamy heat of the day and now bears, beside a second crop of daisies and butter-cups, an ugly harvest of dripping fungus and a prospect of more. In the pain of your helpless bewilderment you remember that tomorrow is Saturday and that you have guests arriving for the week-end.

Dismally, wondering where on earth and perhaps where in hell your wife is, you attack the desperate and uncongenial tasks of watering, ventilating, spraying and, in final desperation, mowing the lawn. Your wife, for some inscrutable reason, does not appear. You have not eaten since midday and now, drenched in sweat, have lost all desire and appetite to do so. A certain savagery, accompanied by pure weakness, takes hold of you, resolving itself into stupefied hatred as you push the heavy mower through the thick, September haylike grass. By the time you have finished the lawn your hands are trembling and there is a certain constriction, followed by a palpitating and repetitive nausea, about the region of the heart. Your tongue lolls out weakly and your whole body has such a shaken and imbecile weakness about it that you cannot even push the mower into the potting-shed.

As you stagger into the house, trying to decide whether bed, bath or brandy would do you the more good, your wife comes in.

'Oh! You've *done* the lawn!'

You cannot answer. It is not that anger, resentment or even disappointment prevent you. A creeping conviction that you may have injured yourself internally is supported by the fact that your stomach seems to have wrapped itself round your left lung. A slight feeling of martyrdom accompanies it, to be increased as you detect a certain unnatural gaiety in the way your wife throws off her hat and gloves, so that you realize vaguely that there has, somewhere, been a party in the air.

'At the Williamsons! I forgot every word about it until Mrs Brownlow phoned.'

Again, afflicted by successive waves of nausea and a sensation of chill from your drying sweat, you cannot answer. Again it is not out of any notion of vindictiveness; you simply cannot see straight; but your wife chooses this moment to say:

'You didn't mind that I went to the party, did you? After all.'

'Greenhouse – everything dead – promised mow lawn.' Waves of sickness, nausea and a recurrent cleavage of the tongue prevent you from going on. Your wife, full of cooling and no doubt stimulating refreshment, now reminds you that she has had a busy day.

'I was rushing about till five o'clock. I hadn't a minute to live. I simply couldn't do everything.'

'Promised mow.'

She cuts you short with a killing, astonishing statement:

'I am not a cart-horse,' she says. 'I can't be expected to run house and garden as well. I can't do *everything*.'

'Promised mow.'

'Yes, but I'm not a *slave*. You could have caught the earlier train.'

'Done now,' you say. 'Finished – brandy – get a bath.'

Estranged and weary and speechless at last, you go to bed.

It is curious that these brave and reckless notions of attempting to run the garden yourself always coincide with the year's most prolific and difficult seasons, autumn and spring. Of these autumn, wet and warm, is most difficult. Sun and rain and storm and sheer sappiness begin to make the garden, by October, a luxuriant and seeding wilderness. Grass grows too fast for the mower; the days grow shorter. There is a great deal to be done that never gets done and soon, by November, afternoons are dark and borders ugly with the slimey wetness of frost on dahlias and zinnias and all that was lovely in summer. There is a great stormy falling of leaves, to sweep which is a Canute-like game, futile and hopeless, made worse after Atlantic storms and maddening wind; and soon the garden is like a frowsy old woman, all uncombed hair and rats' tails, past caring or caring for, ugly and infuriating and depressing to a point where you are glad to draw the curtains early of an evening, with the old country conscience-appeasing benediction: 'Let's shut it out.'

It is on a day such as this, when you are finally prepared to let winter put its claws on your ruin and keep it and do what it will with it until March, that your wife says there's a man in the garden and she thinks he's looking for you. The fact that some stranger or other is always wandering about the garden with the uninvited purpose of taking photographs, selling you your fiftieth insurance policy, merely snooping, begging subscriptions or simply 'Couldn't find nobody at 'ome so I jist wandered round,' is something that helps to keep you unexcited. After some minutes you go into the garden and there, waiting among the late year's leafy and awful ruin, of which you are suddenly most ashamed, is a man, a young man in respectable brown suit, brown shoes and Sunday collar and tie.

This, though you do not yet know it, is your new man. This, in your moment of extreme need, is Mr Dolittle, *the* successor to Mr Pimpkins.

''Ear you ain't got no gardener.'

No, you say, and very guardedly, for the time being, no, you've got no gardener. It has been your fixed intention, indeed, not to have a gardener and to say so, when the need arises, firmly, finally and without fuss. You detest so-called gardeners, and are tired of them. You are about to announce this when you observe that Mr Dolittle is staring with pitying scorn at the frosty ruin of borders, the stormy wreckage of leaf and bough and muck that lies everywhere on beds and paths and lawns. It is all too obvious that he thinks it frightful, as in fact it is, and you yourself are doubly ashamed. Mr Dolittle is, however, too polite to say so and merely delivers, instead, a masterpiece of withering understatement.

'Git on top on y' fore s' long, wun it?'

As it is all too obvious that it has already got on top of you there is very little you can reply to this. You decide to pretend that the dreadful ruin visible everywhere is, after all, a seasonal thing, something to be expected, the mere natural result of summer's end that can and will be cleared up in no time.

Mr Dolittle then says:

'Allus the same, though, en it, this time o' year?'

The note of this observation is not pity; it is not quite comfort; but in some subtle way it displays an understanding of your afflictions. It indicates, clearly, that the condition of your garden is not unique; it even suggests that there may be others who suffer in exactly the same way as you do from autumn's ravages. And indeed Mr Dolittle goes so far as to say so:

'Everybody's in the same pickle. Ent bin able touch nothing. En arf bin some weather en it?'

You agree. Appalling; a discouraging, dreadful year.

'Never 'ad no summer,' Mr Dolittle says, 'did we? Don't sim git no summer nowadays, do we?' And then, with that special brand of semi-biblical cheerful gloom at which countrymen, even young countrymen, so excel:

'Well, it says in the Bible, don' it? Says when the world's comin' t' end, we sharn't know summer from winter, don't it? Sharn't know the changing o' the seasons. Sharn't know.'

'Were you looking for work?'

This abrupt descent from the exclusive plane of biblical parallels down to the plain hard facts of the moment is one that takes Mr Dolittle suddenly off-guard. But not for long.

'Well, I wur and I wurn't. If you see what I mean.'

You make no indication whether you do or not; but Mr Dolittle is kind enough to explain:

'I bin arter a job with a cottage. But I sharn't know nothing definite fer about a fortnit. So while I'm waiting I could come and give y' bit of a clean-up, if you like, bit of a square-round for the winter.'

This, of course, is precisely what you have been looking for. In a few days the scum can be cleared off the lawn and the borders, and soon everything will look reasonably civilized for winter. Without betraying immense enthusiasm, since you have not lived in the countryside for twenty years without knowing some of the tricks, you agree that a quick square-round for the winter might well be a possible thing.

When could Mr Dolittle come?

'Well, I carn't come tomorrer and I carn't come Wednesday.'

Today is Monday. You had somehow formed the impression that Mr Dolittle had two clear weeks of spare time on his hands. Not at all; Mr Dolittle goes on to explain that 'he carn't come Thursday either.'

'Givin' th' ole bus a de-coke.'

Bus?

'Second-hand job. Jis bought it at a sale. Wants a de-coke and some new rings and she'll be like new.'

This is indeed something new: the young, up-to-date gardener with a car. Because of this simple fact Mr Dolittle seems now to be much nearer your world. With Mr Pimpkins, rooted in old and bigoted ways, you were never really at home, and Mr Pimpkins was never really at home with you.

'Handy with cars?' you say.

'Ain't much I carn't do.'

You talk for some minutes of the merits and demerits of various cars, and Mr Dolittle reveals great enthusiasm for the car you possess. Great possibilities begin to suggest themselves: perhaps Mr Dolittle can wash the car, blow up the tyres, change the oil for you. But you are wise enough to check yourself from sailing away on these unlimited dreams, and you say:

'Well, when do you think you could come along?' You want to add 'if at all' and profoundly wish you had done so when Mr Dolittle generously says:

'Well, I'll see if I carn't fit y' in Sat'day morning.'

This seems very cheese-paring treatment from a man who only a few moments before had a fortnight on his hands, but you let it go. It is all well in keeping with the trend, common especially in the south country, that raises every simple act of work or service into the category of a favour conferred. So it will be Saturday, and Mr Dolittle's parting words are:

'I expect y' ain't got no motor mower?'

No: regretfully you have no motor mower.

'Well,' Mr Dolittle says, looking with extreme pity at the hay-like lushness of your lawn, 'gotta git it chewed orf somehow. I'll bring mine.'

So Mr Dolittle makes his casual entry into your service, armed with his own car, his own motor mower, his own tools and a keen interest in all labour-saving devices, such as those fearsome hydra-headed monsters that reap, mow, plough, sow, cut hedges, spray fruit and lime-wash the pig-sty.

'You wanna git one o' them,' Mr Dolittle says, 'they don' arf save the work.'

As you have long been convinced that all labour-saving machines, by the very fact of their expensive existence, make work rather than save it, you resist this significant suggestion of Mr Dolittle's with all the indifference you can muster.

Soon Mr Dolittle's fortnight is up. The first week he has graciously squeezed a day and a half for you; the second week two days and a half. Something has been done to restore the garden's decency, but not really very much. A great deal remains to be done. But there it is: Mr Dolittle is off to his job with the cottage and you propose to pay for his time and tools, thank him and say good-bye.

'Give y' three days next week if y' like,' Mr Dolittle says. 'Ain't got quite so much on.'

'Very well,' you say, 'but wasn't there some talk of a job with a cottage?'

'Fell through,' Mr Dolittle says.

There is a certain darkness about this statement and you say you are sorry.

'I ain't.'

There is nothing to be said to this. It is for you simply to wait for Mr Dolittle, who goes on:

'En arf on the make-haste, some on 'em.'

And with that dark inscrutable comment on the grasping nature of employers Mr Dolittle closes the chapter.

The next is yours. Gradually, insidiously, always with that air of conferring a great favour, with his constant 'I'll see if I can fit y' in another day,' Mr Dolittle comes to you a little more each week until, somewhere about the turn of the year, he has settled himself in for the winter. There is now a great stoking up of greenhouse fires and Mr Dolittle can be found there, under the glass, every morning at nine-thirty and again every afternoon at three o'clock, in the true Pimpkins' manner, 'evvin' me bit o' grub.' It is notable, at this time, how much work there is to be found in the greenhouse and how little, in spite of the hangover of autumnal chaos, in the garden outside. Now and then you suggest that a bit of straight-forward healthy digging might not be out of place, an idea Mr Dolittle counters with the suggestion that he is surprised 'you don' git one o' them tools. They don' arf save the labour.' He even knows where there is one for sale, cheap, second-hand, and he is not at all sure he won't get it himself, ''fore s' long. That is if you don' want it. I could git it cheap for you.' You, however, do not want it, cheap or otherwise, and sure enough, in due course, Mr Dolittle does get it for himself. He is now in possession of a remarkable range of labour-saving instruments and is generally, it is obvious, far better off than you are. He is indeed a worthy modern successor to Mr Pimpkins: for whereas Mr Pimpkins was merely steeped in the pig-headed prejudices of his generation, such as not sowing onions until the end of March or planting potatoes on Good Friday, so that your vegetables were always just enough behind his own to enable him to sell you a few at fancy prices, Mr Dolittle is bound by a whole set of mechanical and state-ordered prejudices peculiar to his time. No doubt, in his youth, Mr Pimpkins worked hard for very little. But Mr Dolittle, who earlier threw out the intimidating reminder that when I worked 'up at the mansion they paid all me insurance,' wants to work a little for a lot. You do indeed, in your own generous foolish way, pay all his insurance, by which his life is state-coddled, as if he were some sort of semi-crippled invalid instead of a healthy Englishman, from the cradle to the grave. It is indeed your fond idea, on the principle of one good turn deserving another, that this extra generosity of yours will cause to be given back, in return, a little extra pull, a little extra heart and sometimes, if needed, a little extra time. But Mr Dolittle, in true modern spirit, is a worker to the clock. In the entire history of labour on the land he is the supreme example of the labourer giving back, to the exact second and the exact halfpenny, the measure of his hire.

Soon spring, with its rising pressure of work, begins to unfold. The comfortable winter, which has also been a dry easy winter, is past. But somehow the garden is never quite what it should be. There is, as it were, always a little piece of pudding left for tomorrow; the work is never quite eaten up. The success and beauty of a garden at a particular time depend to some considerable extent not on the work done at that period but on the work done six months before. A little extra pull is needed in autumn to make sure of a spring glory, and a little extra in spring to make sure of summer. You hope Mr Dolittle is going to give this; it has been expensive and sometimes tiresome to keep Mr Dolittle going throughout the winter and you have only done so because you will need him a hundred times more urgently in spring.

Far from this happening you begin to observe, in April, that Mr Dolittle is beginning to leave the garden at four o'clock in the afternoon. You resist investigating this puzzling change of habit for some days only to discover, presently, that Mr Dolittle is working with scorching energy, every evening, on the lawns of various neighbours. He is also working, in the same way, on Saturdays and Sundays. In winter he managed to put in, for your benefit and at your expense, a forty-eight hour week. Now you make a little calculation and discover it has fallen to forty. At the same time, at the great season of making hay while the sun shines, he is putting in about thirty hours of overtime for over people. For all this you are providing insurance at the crippling rate of twenty-five pounds a year while others escape scot free. Slowly, painfully, sickeningly, you grasp that you have been taken for a mug.

So on a warm spring day, with the garden once again, in Mr Dolittle's own words, 'gittin' on top on y',' you tax Mr Dolittle with what seems to be a slight injustice even in our new state-ordered world. To put it reticently, you feel Mr Dolittle is cheating. The game is not being played. Mr Dolittle is one of a whole army of countrymen who are supplementing their incomes, all summer, at the rate of twenty-five or thirty hours of pay each week, tax free. The simple countryman, unlike the townsman who will not work a second's overtime if he can help it because taxes will make him worse off rather than better, steadily pockets all he earns. No longer has he a straw in his mouth and a jellified, gormless look in his simple eye. He has learned the tricks of State. He has learned to make on the roundabout and cheat on the swings. He wants the smooth, which includes the benefits, but not the rough, which includes the taxes that provide the benefits. He is, after all, just a child of human nature.

But Mr Dolittle does not, or cannot, see these things. He has the proper pig-headed, unanswerable country reply to it all:

'It's me own toime, en it?' he says. 'I can do what I like with me own toime, carn't I?'

He can, and you suggest he does. Useless for you to argue with Mr Dolittle that the success of the communal State depends on whether everybody, including people like himself, play to the rules. He is the new type of countryman, product of war, uneasy peace and welfare Statecraft, mechanized and mean and smart, the up-to-date rural parasite feeding on the fading class to which you yourself still manage to belong. Strange to think that only fifty years ago his father, cap in hand, unblessed with cards of insurance and identity and benefits for this and that, was part of a system which gave us, more especially in this southern county, so much of the beauty of our landscape of woodland and park and great estate: a system of which now only the faded Tchechovian twilight remains.

6 *The Face of Summer*

After the long wet winter and the dark vicious spring, with days of April and May as cruel as January, summer suddenly pretends to unfold itself in a single day of cloud-cleared sky and softening wind. The morning is cool and fresh, with slow-rolling pillows of pure white cloud. At first they thicken, breezily, with undershadows of bluish-grey, and then noon seems to lift them up, blowing them gently apart until presently they are like high flying feathers, and then by afternoon like long combed-out strands of sparse white hair, stretching trans-parently far across blue sky. Our horizons here, because of trees and the rolling nature of the land, are never wide: we cannot see the long westerly sweep of weald, with its sea-borne storms and fire-golden sunsets, because of high folds of beeches on the collar of a hill. But on a day like this, with a sky always lifting until it is really lofty and far away by late afternoon, the horizon itself gives the illusion of widening, creating a sense of gentle expansiveness, to which some reflection of sunlight gives a wonderful air of clarity. By afternoon too the wind stills down, and the air, warming every moment, becomes in a curious way hollow rather than quiet, a sort of glass bell in which the voices of birds keep up a high sustained vibration of echoing sweetness, a thing especially true of stuttering cuckoos and the deep round-blown notes of blackbirds.

On such afternoons of still, bird-sweet warmth the incomparable spell of this stretch of countryside begins to cast itself magically. You feel it in both sky and earth, from the high combed-out cloud down to the field-mouse that comes jumping over the lawns like a miniature kangaroo to feed, with nibblings of white crumbs, on a skinned crocus bulb. He stays there for quite some time, unconcerned, intent as a child on an apple, dropping crocus crumbs as he quivers hungrily in the sun. He is somehow, for me, a truer symbol of the day's May-time quietness, utterly without treachery at last, than even the chorus of blackbirds and the rare stuttering, choking cuckoo. During his meal among the crocuses, two inches from my feet, I have a short conversation with him; but again, exactly like any child, he is too absorbed to make any kind of movement in answer. It is only when I speak to him a little louder, as it were sharply, that he drops a last scared crumb and with his bounding kangaroo-like leaps, tiny feet exposed like grey pedals at the back, disappears into the sword-forest of yucca leaves.

Before this, and again after he has gone, the enchantment of the afternoon is made more full by the behaviour of a pair of gold-finches. Indeed there are two pairs, quite a rarity for this garden, and both are nesting. Whether goldfinches are more specially affectionate than other birds I don't know, but both pairs escort each other about the garden with the closest and most delicately fussy attention, never more than a few inches away from each other, as if joined together by a piece of invisible string. It seems always as if the flight of one, prinking and excited, is pulling the other away. One pair has already finished building, high in a golden cypress, and the others now and then disappear in a dual flutter of yellow and crimson over the house, where they are probably building in a clump of higher darker macrocarpa.

They are greatly attracted, about this time, by a bed of forget-me-nots, deep blue, from which rise tulips in ten or fifteen heights and colours, tawny bishop's purple to white, orange to delicate rose. The goldfinches pay several visits here, looking round. The bed is raised up, built between thick cheese-green lumps of Kentish ragstone, and the gold-finches twitter nervously about these stone boundaries, peering into the blue forest of flower, as if this is exclusive and forbidden territory. Several times they look as if they are going in, but each time, excited and nervous, they pull each other away and, in a sort of prancing flight, disappear. Every few moments they are back again and finally, at the pitch of child-like tension, one disappears into the forget-me-nots while the other, exactly like a child keeping watch on the edge of an orchard, stays quivering outside. Out comes the first, eventually, with a minute blue spray of forget-me-not in its mouth and both, in a scramble of hysterical excitement, gold and crimson heads close together and now brilliantly touched with blue, dash away nestwards to use their flower.

The day ends with such an expanse of cleared blue sky and with such choruses of bird song that summer at last seems to have settled itself down, as it did in France a month ago, like a contented broody hen. The house martins, throughout the day, have been flying higher and higher – in a whole host of country weather adages this, in my experience, is about the only accurate portent of improving weather – and on one occasion a robin comes down to the lawn and from under the showering pink cherry, so glorious all day against the deep blue sky, selects a fallen petal for himself, in emulation of the goldfinches, and flies away with it in his mouth to the bank under the oak trees across the field. The evening air, though cooling a little, is clotted with the scent of wallflowers and there is a sheen on the tulips, especially the plum-like purples and cherry crimsons, that is exactly like the bloom of fruit-skins in pristine ripeness. Lilac has sprung into bloom and in the house a solitary rose, a *Gloire de Dijon*, fattens its first pink and ivory buds. A tree creeper slithers up and down the limbs of the willow tree more nervously than ever the field-mouse did in the warm afternoon and across the field, at long last, weeks late, the horse-chestnuts are in unruffled and perfect flower.

You need only walk out now to see the apple orchards in full glory to satisfy yourself that summer has come at last, in all its balmy, thickening blessedness, to this spell-bound piece of country. There is a tendency, earlier in the year, to make pilgrimages into Kent in order to worship at cherry orchard shrines, and there is no doubt that, in April, the cold lace-like whiteness of cherries, stretched over sheep-grazed hillsides, is a lovely thing. But it is not until May, when apple orchards come bursting into full-clustered bloom, every bough solid with rose-bud pink and white, sometimes deep crimson, that the real orchard grandeur comes to lift the entire countryside out of its pallid half-wintry greenness with the effect of illumination. No cherry can possibly compare with it, and even the recollection of peach orchards in blossom fades, for all its beauty, against this solid and yet airy splendour, so friendly and yet so aristocratic. There is no counting our orchards here; they go on and on; every year there are more and more of them; every year they are, I think, more intelligently kept, more shapely and more prodigious in flower; every year there is always somebody – so that now they are beginning to say we have far too many orchards and that soon there will be no profit in it – ready to plant another. To which I can only say damn the profit; someone will one day show me a starving Kentish fruit farmer, lean no doubt from years of crawling under his bed to count his money, and then I shall believe, at last, that orchards are no longer wanted in this fair, rich county.

So after a day of settled and enchanting warmth, made rich by the happy behaviour of two goldfinches and a robin with flowers in their mouths and a field-mouse with the bulb of a flower in his, it is possible to go to bed with a feeling of relaxation, of no longer feeling tautened and on edge against east wind, a delightful sensation of being almost securely embalmed by the full fragrant tenderness of a world of blue-bells and apple-blossom and bird-song and rainless cloud. The face of summer is visible at last; the year has settled down.

In the morning a sky the colour of an ill-used dishcloth hangs where the pure canopy of yesterday's afternoon uplifted, with its clear blueness, the pale green of fresh oak-flower, turning it almost to the yellow of a daffodil. A storm of the old dark vicious-ness, of which every other day for a year seems to have given an example, comes riding in, beating and glowering, from the Atlantic. The lawn, thick with pale cherry petals, has the appearance of a wet church-yard after a wedding. The tulips hang cringing away. Soon the sour sad sound of wind in half-leafed boughs, rising with successive moans, takes away all but the most persistent of bird-song. Rain has fallen heavily, cooling the air, but the wind is so strong that the drops beaded earlier on every twig, dry quickly. We are half-way back to winter. As the day advances the only things that do not seem to mind all this are the birds, and the blackbirds are so clamorous that they are almost defiant in the rising wind. The goldfinches continue to go hand-in-hand, in their attentive affectionate fashion, all over the garden, stealing sprigs of forget-me-not flower, scratching for shreds of something too minute to see from the bark of the willow. A robin comes again to the cherry petals and a pair of blue tits, in one of those ecstatic frenzies of mating passion that shake the fragile blue frame like an electric shock, come together for a second or two in the green catkins and then disappear.

The night falls cold; but next morning, wholly unexpected, there is sudden boiling sultriness everywhere. It seems as if earth and grass are heating up under your feet; there is a magical flaring of buttercups in the brilliance of brief flashes of thundery sun. The first tree of roses, the lovely Chinese *Hugonis*, with its pretty pinnate leaves and its exquisite yellow buttons of single blossom, is in full bloom, throwing out arching wands, gracefully, in weeping fashion. There is a scarlet-orange flash of the first poppy, too brilliant against the restrained cool tulips that has opened in the night. A bird that has been silent far too long in the dark cold weather, the turtle dove, sets up once again a summery strumming in the flowering oaks, perfectly in tune with a day that grows sleepier and sultrier without ever breaking to full sun. By afternoon you can see that not a single candle of chestnut blossom remains un-opened; yet there is not a single sprig of May-blossom anywhere – only, on every tree, in every wood and roadside, an astonishing thickening, almost a curdling, of greenness in the thundery air. By evening in fact, the air is so hot and close that, at dinner, sweat breaks out thickly on my face and a friend gazes at me with a sort of dry sadness and says: 'My dear fellow, you look as if you will not keep long in this weather.'

By morning a storm of terrifying and astonishing magnificence has gathered in the west. It suddenly presents itself in the shape of a colossal slate-grey glacier, filling the entire western sky and giving the impression of being part of a mountainside that is about to slide to earth. It curves in a defined smooth ridge of solid grey, below which deeper and deeper cloud folds in dark blue contortions, in a sort of intestinal knottiness. For about ten minutes, about eight o'clock, there is an increasing dry blowing of rainless wind. It roars sea-like across the folds of fields and all at once it seems as if, sea-fashion, it drives huge bursts of yellow sea-spray through the oak trees. After some moments it becomes clear that this is, after all, not spray, but dust. Its fineness, its particular yellowness and the fact that it is to be seen nowhere but on the leeward side of the oaks are things that make it, for a few moments, mystifying. It is only after some time, after the third or fourth cloud has gone whirling down-wind, that it becomes clear that this is a mass of blown oak-pollen, fine as sulphur and about the same colour, that the storm is whipping and scattering from the enormous trees of flower.

By nine o'clock there is darkness on earth. Fat black drops of rain, twice as large as pennies, flop on paths. The glacier, resolving itself, expanding, rushing eastward, is no longer a glacier but a complete iron lid through which there suddenly bursts, with simultaneous splendour and terror, a crack of blue flame releasing a petrifying blast of thunder without a second's delay. This blast, it turns out, strikes a nearby oak, a giant whose bark is skinned off in deep crude tears, as if it were cheap shoe leather. Presently the sky becomes too dark for even the weird brilliance of oak and chestnut to be seen; the trees are drowned in waterspouts of black rain. Yet all through this phenomenon of moving darkness, with its fierceness of blue lightning and simultaneous thunder and far-bounding echoes, the birds everywhere grow more magnificent in an unconcerned chorus of song.

Indeed the storm seems, if anything, to excite them; they are exalted and clamorous, exactly as if wanting to make themselves heard above the stunning jabber of the storm. Most curious of all of them is the turtle dove, silent so long through the crippling easterly winds, and now stimulated by rain and darkness and thunder to his true, moaning, summery loveliness of voice, the notes repeated and repeated low in the background of storm like a velvety echo.

By ten o'clock rain has washed every sign of violence from the air. Not a leaf moves. The heads of all the pink tulips are curved over with drooping swan-like grace, revealing at the back of their necks a star of pure and exquisite blue. Birds calm down, not completely, but for brief intervals, creating a feeling of wonderfully serene hushed calm. The air seems softer, warmer than ever, and as the trees dry themselves there begins a slow sound of rain-drops plopping and slopping on drenched paths and grass; and then at last, quite rapidly, there is a clearing of cloud from the west, revealing a pale egg-blue sky scribbled with small white cloud and giving, suddenly, a brilliance of bursting sun that sets air and tree and grass and flower pulsating with a delicious scintillation of perfect summer light.

The effect of long spells of unchanged weather is such as to cheat, in a way, your sense of recollection. So many days, whether raining or fine, have been the same that it is hard to look back and say, with clear conviction, which was one and which the other. This is more true of tropical climates, where day after day of sunlight has the effect, ultimately, of telescoping time, giving it also the illusion of passing very quickly; but it is also true, in England, of long spells of dreary wetness with which winter, in 1951, has just ended.

So it seems a long time, years instead of a few months, since the first tulip was in bloom. It opened on January the 18th: not a freak, not indeed a particularly brilliant or gorgeous thing, but a very precious magenta-coloured creature about as large as a medium-sized fuchsia – the species *pulchella,* in its variety *Violet Queen.* It rises from twisted green and coppery leaves, only an inch or two from the ground, at a time when aconites and snowdrops are likely to be its only other flowering companions, unless you have been wise in the matter of crocus species, by which time your rewards will be carpets of mauve and yellow and orange glory. I shall say much more of these crocus species in a later chapter; they are quite unparalleled in their December and January beauty, giving flowers without fail at Christmas or even before, so that incredulous visitors may be taken before the turn of the year and shown such a species as *laevitigus* in all its rich delicacy, in full bloom, with crowds of stencilled mauve and orange stars. But the tulip species begin almost as early and go on much later, the last of them coming in late May or early

June, so that they have a season of nearly half the year. As bulbs they are not, perhaps, very long-lived; they do not increase, as the crocus do, by the sowing of thousands of little grass-like seedlings everywhere; but their rather brief infertile lives are full of such unseasonable splendour that every gardener ought to pawn his soul, if necessary, in order to try a few dozens of them every year. The surprising thing is that very few gardeners do.

The immediate response to the fact that we have tulips in bloom in January, in the open air, is one that assails us regularly in the south country. 'Oh! yes, but you're *earlier*,' friends say, 'you're *warmer*. You're awfully *sheltered*, aren't you?' It so happens that we are not particularly sheltered and that Kent is, on the whole, a coldish county, especially in spring, when easterly winds of a particularly refined ruthlessness spill over barer stretches of northern downs with the effect of glacial waterfalls. The flowering of tulip species has, in fact, nothing to do with the earliness of this county or any other; yet it is very hard indeed to persuade gardeners north of London that it is so. *Pulchella Violet Queen* is supposed to flower in January, or at latest in February, and most years it does so. There is nothing freakish about it. Yet every year, when I write down for gardening friends its name and that of its far lovelier successors, the brilliant beauties of February and March, I see always a look of curious incredulity in their eyes. It is as if I am giving them the names of impossibly exotic orchids which in their hearts they know they cannot grow. They murmur absently about protection and speak of providing shelter by cloches; and when I meet them a year later and ask if their tulips proved to be the winter enchantments I said they would I see only the old pitying look of faint martyrdom in their eyes which says: 'It's all very well for you. You're that much farther south. You're warmer. You're so beautifully sheltered. They'd never do with us.'

I am not therefore going to preach to the reader on the earliness, the hardiness and the incomparable beauty of tulip species; I will simply say that for the price of two theatre stalls for a bad play and the price of a bad meal before or after it you can buy yourself a few dozen bulbs of half a dozen varieties that will turn out, without fail, to be heavenly things. You should start, I think, with *pulchella*, sometimes called the crocus-tulip, of which the hybrid *Violet Queen* is a little earlier than the type, and, even if not absolutely queenly, is of such beauty and early hardiness that its upturned fuchsia-liked blossoms are quite startling on the January earth, among their crinkled leaves, in the wintry air. You will have to wait a fortnight, perhaps three weeks, just possibly a month, for its immediate successor, *Kaufmaniana*, the water-lily tulip, of which there are now twenty or more hybrid varieties, varying from almost pure ivory to scarlet-orange, with intermediate ranges of markings and shapes that never quite lose the original water-lily character of the clean pure flower opening flat in the sun.

The original *Kaufmaniana,* is still one of the loveliest and earliest, is the colour of butter, with outer petal markings of pink that vary between salmon and a tender cherry-rose. I have never yet decided, and I do not think anyone else ever has, whether the closed flower, like a narrow and slender goblet of butter with pink veinings, is more beautiful than the full-open flower that floats on its glaucous green leaves exactly like the water-lily that gives it its name. I do not think there is any deciding. It is simpler, perhaps, to be grateful for these two wonders, exactly as you are grateful for the beauty of both old and young wine: purely on the principle that if life offers the choice of two fountains it is better to drink at both. *Kaufmaniana* will anyway open with the sun and close with cloud: so that every day, perhaps half a dozen times day, you will have the good fortune to be able to see one or the other or both these beautiful characteristics. It ought to bloom, I think, for about three weeks, in which time it will have been overtaken by any number of its hybrids, of which *Scarlet Elegance,* a startling and exotic flame, pure colour both inside and out, is as exciting as a firework in the dark days of February. It will have been preceded, also, by several others, including one called *The First,* supposedly three weeks earlier than the type, a refined hybrid of ivory and stripes of red strawberry. The hybrids of *Kaufmaniana* are every year increasing so fast in number that only the millionaire, paying pounds for single bulbs of new varieties, can keep up with them. But every one I have seen has been beautiful; all have the purity and warmth so charac-teristic of the parent, not the least of whose virtues is a perfection of dignity and grace without a touch of vulgarity; and there are now shades of copper-rose and pink-sienna and cherry-gold that, ten years ago, were quite unknown. It is possible therefore to have five or six weeks of *Kaufmaniana* and its fantastic family: from early February to mid-March at least and probably later, the time varying a week or two either way according to the caprice of spring.

Once *Kaufmaniana* has started there is a sudden rush of tulip species to wake the whole of March and April with a flamboyance that, as Farrer said, blazes so savagely 'at the end of Spring that eye can scarcely bear the furnaces of their vast expanded flowers under the sun.' This is utterly true of *Fosteriana* that is quite unequalled in all the range of tulip species and indeed, I fancy, in the whole gardening year. Not even oriental poppies or dahlias can quite equal this flaunting emperor of blossom, anything from six to nine inches across, the absolute potentate of all spring. The species *Eichleri*, on narrow grey-green leaves that have something of the tender bloom of a June pea-pod, is like a rather smaller but still brilliant and exquisite version of it; a sort of black and scarlet prince among the blowsy potentates. I like

Eichleri, of which there is now a larger version called *Excelsa,* very much; and then there are two species, *praestans* and *turkestanica,* which are not satisfied with producing one tulip, in the general fashion, on a stem, but which branch out into candelabra, scarlet in the case of *praestans,* creamy-white in the case of *turkestanica.* These are beautiful too: though not more beautiful than our own wild tulip, *sylvestria,* so like a butter-yellow fritillary with its drooping elegant heads when it flowers in April. The yellow of tulips, touched by a suspicion of green, is always superbly refined, without harshness, and gardeners who like curious things, of unobvious enchantment, might try the species *vivid-iflora,* already a great favourite with those schools of flower decorators who create odd confections out of rhubarb, cabbage and seakale.

Vividiflora is a crimped and twisted creature – the species *cornuta stenopetala* outdoes it altogether by being the crooked witch of all tulips, with hawk-like talons of quite human weirdness in scarlet and yellow – that is nearly pure green. There is just enough of a feathering of yellow to give the petals life and altogether it is a distinct and charming addition to the whole curious family of green flowers, in which the old auriculas, ringed with black and lime, and that strange iris, *tuberosa,* with its green and black orchids in April, are the best known aristocrats, and lords-and-ladies and spurge-laurel the commonest. *Vividiflora* is, indeed, beautiful; it has also the virtue of flowering late and, perhaps because of its leaf-like flowers, of lasting long.

But in this curious year of Grace, 1951, which will surely go down as a freak of prolonged coolness, producing as it did hardly a day with a temperature of 70° until early July, all tulips were long-lasting. In mid-June, in slightly shaded spots, they were flowering side by side, unblemished, with the first house-roses, which in turn were to prolong their own first flowering for several weeks, instead of a mere hand-span of days, as in hotter years: so that now, in the first week of July, the aristocratic *Lady Hillingdon*, with hanging flowers of deep apricot, is just as beautiful as she was a month ago, when the last tulips seemed as if they might flower on through summer. Beside her the shyer trees of *Etoile d'Hollande* and *Lady Sylvia* have already faded; but *Lady Hillingdon*, the perfection of all house-roses, blending so beautifully with stone and brick and that rose-sienna tile of which the south country is full, simply trails and spreads her slender coppery branches until she is an immense fan of leaf and bud and swinging flower. The garden is now, in fact, all rose, all scent, all loveliness. From the pergola the great pure mass of *Easlea's Golden Rambler*, powerful in growth and flower and perfume, flaunts up in a glorious yellow tangle in which pale violet clematis twist like lovely accidents, with the startling effect of revolutionary mauve roses growing from the masses of shining briar. The big perfect cabbages of *La France* and *Lemon Pillar* fall in their full blooming, like pink and ivory snowballs, bursting and lighting up the shade below, each petal doomed and perfect as it lies fresh in the moment of falling among the budding fuchsia trees. Occasionally the lightest stir of wind peels away a single petal that floats down gently like a lazy saucer. A little rain brings down a whole storm of broken flower, so that every day or two the shady tunnel of the pergola is thick with yellow and pink and white and crimson petals, all the ripe showering of high summer falling soundlessly under rain and breeze and sun and lovely in its falling.

In a few weeks the fuchsias will be in bloom. At first we had only a dozen or two of them, nourishing and nurturing and coddling them under glass, repotting and shading and feeding them as if they were semi-exotic creatures, which in their exceptional beauty they certainly are. But it is in the nature of fuchsias to grow quickly and to propagate readily; and soon the plants in thumb-pots were trees in twelve-inch pots; the greenhouse was a forest of expanding fuchsia umbrellas; and our few dozen plants grew to fifty and then to a hundred and then to three or four hundred, presenting us with the impossible problem of either throwing them away or building a glass-house of magnificent proportions in order to house them. Both these things being quite impossible we decided to disobey former practice, which was not very extensive anyway, and plant our fuchsias outside. The results in the depressing summer of 1950, another freak year of cool darkness and Atlantic storms, were wonderful. The fuchsias revelled in the prolonged cool wetness and were only taken up in November, still in full flower, because frost threatened. Frost, in fact, did more than threaten; before we could house them properly and safely for the winter a vicious snap of twenty degrees caught them with unexpected ruthlessness, freezing them solid and black in their pots: to which their ultimate answer, in spring, was a fine and healthy breaking of new leaf, with only an odd casualty among the older trees.

The fancies and tastes of gardeners are curious things. The darlings of Edwardian days are suddenly despised by a generation which exerts itself prodigiously to grow thimble-like campanulas of short-lived grace among rocks as big as railway wagons. Things like auriculas and fuchsias and petunias and pelargoniums are rejected as being either too difficult or as being part of an era in which plush, large buttonholes and high bosoms were over-revered. There is a tendency, in some quarters, to despise begonias or to talk of herbaceous borders as being like the tie-shops of the Burlington Arcade. There is an arch-priesthood of alpinism, in which all mention of orchids is heresy. Yet the yearly exhibit of crusty ravines stabbed with neat pockets of primula and saxifrage continually shown with such pains at Chelsea already seems to me as old-fashioned as work in crochet, and it is significant that the most sensational exhibit at the high altar there last year, an arrangement quite stunning in its effect on English gardeners still conservatively wandering among lumps of natural limestone, was an Italian display of cacti. Shades of Miss Jekyll and Mr Robinson, who are about to turn over in their graves, I feel, at a new and revolutionary trend away from Nature.

In all the changes from formality to naturalism in gardening, extending over the past fifty years, the fuchsia has been a casualty. With the pelargonium – which on the island of Madeira, for instance, grows into splendid hedge-like barriers of woody stalk and bright fat leaf, as vigorous as any michaelmas daisy here at home – it has been thrust into the horticultural background not only as a rather suburban Victorian plant but as one rather difficult to keep clean. Certainly, when coddled under glass, it tends to became sticky with aphis, a fly-blown mess. The answer is not to grow it under glass. It does not need heat, and even early spring sunlight will scorch it. In the garden, preferably in partial shade, it will grow with the vigour of dahlias, its flowering time about the same, and it has the useful characteristic, in our climate, of being a sort of semi-herbaceous shrub. This means that you can grow it how you will: as a bedding plant, flowering along with petunias and verbenas, or as a neat shrub, a foot or two high, or with true ambition as a standard or half-standard, umbrella-shaped, so that it makes a delicious hanging canopy of purple and cherry, or white and rose, or mauve and vermilion, in single or double form as the case may be. Many of the hybrid varieties, the doubles especially, are old, dating from the last century, from days when opulence in flowers was not despised. The big crinkled purple double flowers are, in their fresh unfolding, very like the balls of crêpe paper that we made as children by sewing folded segments together. They expand, finally, to the shape of crinolines, revealing underneath tucked and pleated masses of purple or lilac underskirts and glimpses of stamens protruding in several lengths like toes. Lovely and massive and rich though the doubles are, the singles too are of great elegance. The rising star-like petals become, in full expansion, flying and floating things: the long corolla has the effect of a bell with many white-tipped clappers to which bees cling as they climb up and disappear in fuzzy exploration. There is no scent to them; all their beauty is in the exquisite variations of petal, corolla and stamen, played on a few octaves of colour, purple and vermilion and mauve and white providing the dominant shades. A touch of delicate blue, by no means pure but nearer to harebell shade and in itself delicious, appears in some smaller varieties, but there is nothing of delphinium brilliance, and no yellow. There is a variety, and a most beautiful one, called *Swanley Yellow*, which, as someone once pointed out, is certainly not yellow anywhere else, whatever it may be at

Swanley. Its tube is long and of soft orange and it gives the impression of some enlarged darting humming-bird hawk-moth of unusual brilliance rather than a flower.

The procedure with the entire family, is, in our experience, and as with so much else, one of simplicity. On the principle that some people are not happy unless they are exquisitely miserable, so there are gardeners who do not get the best out of the game unless they are permanently bug-conscious and in a constant frenzy of fear about insecticides. I have never had a bug worth worrying about on my fuchsias, which are now put out to fend for themselves, like hardy cattle, in May, and herded into the shelter of the cold house in November, there to rest until they are pruned, exactly like roses, in early spring. From this pruning spring hundreds of fresh shoots, which may be pinched and stopped or left alone or taken for cuttings, according to fancy. Nothing in the world is easier to root than a fuchsia cutting in spring, and it has the added virtue of turning itself into a vigorous flowering bush by September, the month in which the outdoor fuchsia is at its best, especially in those humid mist-laden years of blackberry beauty when nights are warm enough to bring glow-worms out on roadsides. The school of scrubbing and spraying and washing and fussing is not, therefore, one with which we have much sympathy. Fuchsias, not unnaturally perhaps, are in our experience best left alone, to themselves and among themselves, the only exceptions to this procedure being that they respond to continual support with rings and strings and revel in the repeated wash of clear water on their leaves and flowers.

Perhaps the only thing to be said against fuchsias is that sometimes, in cool years, in those odd English summers that become incurably blighted with cool Atlantic cloud, they are so slow to reach their perfection of flower that the threat of frost overtakes them in their full beauty. Gardeners long then, as they wait for the first ugly death-blow of frost at dahlias and petunias and geraniums and begonias, for a climate that is swifter and surer in its summer rise and less deadly in its late autumnal ruin; they ache, I fancy more especially as they grow older, for a climate in which there is no frost, no ugly November blackening, none of that hatred that enters every gardening heart when the first pulpy desolation of winter replaces, overnight, the year's late joys. Every gardener who feels like that – and I confess to a steady deepening hatred of winter and its tomb-like qualities, in which I do not think I am at all alone – ought to see, if only once in his life, the island of Madeira, the general character of whose famous gardens is so like our own, and yet so fantastically unlike them, that it is in all sorts of ways like a piece of England, done in the English taste, with semi-tropical exuberance, more than a thousand miles away. Even so, when you arrive off the bay of Funchal on a brilliant February morning under a sky in which the only clouds are like fuzzy nightcaps on the mountains, there will be no sign of any extraordinary splendour about the island waterfront except a few purple splashes of bougainvillea on black volcanic rocks and the vivid blue and orange scimitars of Van Gogh-like fishing-boats pulled up on a narrow shore of black sand. Here, you might well begin to say to yourself, gazing up at infinite tiers of pink and cream houses built like clean cubes into steep rock, is simply another Monte Carlo, another Palma de Majorca, or just another southern sea-port town. Yet nothing could be more wrong than that first hurried and slightly disappointing impression. Madeira is not Monte Carlo; it is not Majorca, delicious and lovely though that island is; it is not Mediterranean; and, though it lies only three hundred miles from the western coast of Africa, it is not African. And, perhaps oddest of all, it is, though a Portuguese possession, not absolutely Portuguese. It is in fact a remarkable example of English merchant colonization in a territory governed by another and most benevolent flag: a colonization powerful, unobtrusive, fabulous and yet quiet, built up with constant Portuguese assistance, that makes this island, only twenty-five miles long and twelve broad, one of the pleasant phenomena in our modern world.

I want to presume you are going in February not simply because February is the only month when I have been there myself but because February, though not more beautiful than January or March or May, gives the greatest possible joy of contrast to the English visitor who leaves the few sparse snowdrops of his native land to make the thirteen hundred miles journey southward. For the splashes of purple bougainvillea on black rocks are not an accident; and they are in no way singular. They are simply one part of a fantasy, almost a frenzy, of flowers that cover Madeira for almost the whole year and that cover it most luxuriantly in what is charmingly called the Madeira winter.

If you are, like me, an ardent and reasonably experienced traveller, you will have learned, by this time, to be distrustful of the guide book of convention. 'Travellers should take light summer or sub-tropical clothing, with a light wrap for evenings,' you read and at once, with memories of mistrals that strike like cold steel, decide to pack furs and tweeds and a bottle of cough-cure. On this basis it is more than probable that you are about to distrust me. But the plain fact is that when you arrive in Madeira in February you go back, or forward, into summer: not merely a fickle cheating moment of summer, the false breath that brings a chance bee or yellow brimstone out across the lawn at home before the sallow-bud has yellowed, but whole and perfect summer, the summer of July. In case this sounds too simple to be true I will add that this summer is also spring, and if it is not too incredible, early autumn too. As you step from the boat and drive up into the town of enchanting old-walled streets the first splash of magenta bougainvillea on black rocks is suddenly engulfed by immense torrents of colour. There are now, you are able to see, whole acres of bougainvillea, ravines and gorges of purple and crimson and burnt-rose. Cascades of orange-trumpeted bignonia, and another of finer, spark-like scarlet, fall everywhere from high stone walls. Enormous crimson-green stars of poinsettia flash in gardens, on potato patches, on the edges of banana plantations. Bushes of lanata, a verbena-like shrub with chameleon heads of flowers that range from orange to magenta and pink to yellow, are in flower; the bombax is crowded with blossoms like stiff-winged scarlet macaws. Geraniums and wild arum lilies clog the roadside under mimosas and avenues of rose- and peach-coloured hibiscus. Jacarandas – there are probably two or three miles of them about the streets of Funchal – are just beginning to open, at the high tips, their first wistaria-mauve finger-stalls of flower, so fragile and beautiful, and on house-walls and garden fences the wistarias themselves are knotted, silky-grey, in bud.

And in gardens everywhere – those legendary and wonderful gardens that, as I say, the English have done so much to establish and perfect on Madeira – it is July: together with incongruous moments of autumn and spring. Beds of petunia and verbena and snapdragon and marigold and everlasting flower and gerbera daisy and sweet-peas; a splendour of roses in beds and on pergolas; and then suddenly, un-expectedly, the touch of spring – a crowd of violets, dark and fat, heavy with fragrance – and then back to summer, to exoticism, with masses of too-rich, too dazzling cinerarias and whole hedges of cherry-and-black pelargonium; and then back to spring again with a run of daffodils and whole streams of pale yellow freesias, sweet as honey, and then on to autumn with rosy gladioli, slender and purple and wild in the potato patches farther up the hills, a few dahlias and even a chrysanthemum or two; and then back to spring again with white Easter lilies, yellow and crimson ranunculus and even, in the baskets of the flower-girls, a bunch of pink primroses among the shell-like glories of rose camellias. From these flower-girls, with their fawn high boots, yellow and crimson skirts and crimson capes, carrying enormous baskets of blossom on their heads, you may buy fresh freesias and ixias, narcissuses and camellias, and occasional sprays of loveliest wine-brown orchids. For five escudos, about fifteen pence, you can buy a bunch of thirty or forty camellias, a small armful, or a bouquet of freesias and narcissuses and occasionally a bunch of two species of gazania that we never see in England, one beetroot crimson, the other orange-brown, both silver-leaved. For nine pence you can give your girl-friend an orchid; for fifteen shillings you can buy her such a garland of them, as in London or New York, only millionaires could afford.

It may well be that such luxuriance of flowers would, in time, tire or bore you. I have never tired of it myself and since it is always in a process of fairly rapid change it has never bored me. But Madeira, so constructed that it rises in its twelve mile width to heights of 6,000 feet, could anyway adequately take care of such feelings. In half an hour, in a taxi, you can climb out of the region of the sub-tropical. From areas of congested luxuriance where custard apples and guavas and lemons and sugarcane and papaias and yams grow among the bananas you can rise to a world where plums are in blossom and apple trees are as bare as in an English December. It is cooler, but not cold. Geraniums flourish wild in the rock: arum lilies are being cut with a little sparse grass for cattle food; the hill-slopes are lovely with slender eucalyptus and mimosa in yellow bloom. Every garden, however tiny, has its camellia-tree, high as the house, all rosy or white with flower; and all along the roadsides, for miles and miles, endlessly, ribbons of blue agapanthus lily, planted wherever a new strip of road is made, are coming into flower. In April and May these agapanthus, mostly blue, but occasionally white, will be in full glory – while you and I, in England, will be tenderly lifting ours out in pots, for the summer, hoping that August will give us the pleasure of a precious spray or two of flowers.

And then further beyond this, beyond the daffodils and the Chinese primulas in the gardens and the last agapanthus and the last camellias, there is an extraordinary stark wild magnificence. The central valleys, with primitive villages scattered about fishless and shallow streams, have all the splendour of parts of Switzerland and the Dolomites. Dark, volcanic, savage rocks are covered with tree heathers, wild bay-trees, low pines that peasants cut for litter, and flat saucer-like cactus wherever rocks give water. And soon there is nothing up here except a few sheep scratching the upper ledges of pasture, a goat or two and a hovering hawk. The air whips down windy and sharp; it is a world of lonely and lofty magnificence where, if you slip and break your leg on wet rocks, there is no way to hospital except by hammock. From a point here you can see the sea on both north and south coasts – and hardly believe that only a mile or two beyond the odd sheep tracks yams are growing by the river bed and blackbirds singing with splendid May-time richness by the sea.

Up here, halfway between the mountains and the coast, we saw two gardens. At home, in the park, after Mr Kimmins and William and Sam had finished their great clearing-up campaign, we had planted, with reckless ambition, half a dozen camellia-trees. In this enterprise we were justified by the knowledge that in the village, in another park, camellias grew with splendour, slightly sheltered by cypress and laurestinus, to yield in March and April the loveliest rose-pink and rose-striped blossoms. The only camellias we had ever grown, and they too in their modest way were splendid, were in pots, and the inspiration for these had been born in a garden on Lake Como, where camellia-trees grow almost as large as oaks, a luxuriance only equalled in the same garden by purple beds of cherry-pie, on which the heads of blossom were like massed coxcombs of curly kale. But these camellias were not then in bloom, and it was only when we drove up the hillside in Madeira, in late February, that we saw for the first time what camellias can be. Here there were long noble avenues of them: not very tall, not higher than good-sized cherry-trees, perhaps because they had been planted a little too close together, but of a massed and casual splendour that I shall never forget. There were, perhaps, forty or fifty colours or variations of colour, from purest white to a deep glistening rose, not unlike the colour of a Betty Uprichard, with its touch of paler curling pink at the edge. There were stripes and breaks like the featherings in the bizarre tulips of old Dutch paintings; there were serene cool vermilions and fuchsia-like crimsons and one vast variety of clean rich cerise, about as large as a tea-plate and slightly rolled at the edge, in which the queenliness of all camellias reached its utter perfection. And everywhere, on grass, on paths, on flower-beds, the camellias had fallen, as they will, in full beauty, the weight of flowers too much for the short stalk, the delicate petals bruised by falling or by wind. The wheels of the taxi crushed them as we passed and farther down the hill many small boys thrust up to us tight bunches of stolen pure white buds, just breaking, like fat water-lilies offered on platters of laurel-shining leaves.

And then in the garden itself, as if an avenue of camellias were not enough, there were individual trees of broader splendour, with many magnolias of uncommon loveliness. A cool wind was blowing that day, unkindly on the masses of winging dove-like flowers. The grass everywhere was a litter of white and purple petals, like plucked feathers. And in the flower-beds and along the paths two old women, heads hidden in sacks against the wind, were mindlessly and slowly pulling out masses of scented weeds. These weeds, it turned out, were freesias. Common as daisies, despised as dandelions, they were being scratched up everywhere, from flower-beds and the fissures of paths, where they had seeded themselves into tight dwarf carpets, now in delicious blossom. I thought of my few prayed-over sulky seeds of freesia dead in cold pans in the cold house at home; and when I could bear it no longer I walked on among great drifts of orange and yellow and salmon azalea and mists of fragile Chinese primula, about the colour of lady-smocks, and then more freesias, in seeding scented drifts, a wild nuisance everywhere. A Scots nurse, relic of days of Victorian opulence, sat knitting under a Judas tree, a tree I was later to see all over southern France, gracing every roadside with its daphne-flowered leafless branches; but when I asked her the name of another tree, standing above her like an elephant-eared giant weighed down with purple decoration, she said she didna know the names of flowers and then, dour and abrupt, went on knitting, mindless as the old women tugging out the impossible freesias, as if she had nothing to look at but the granite landscape of somewhere like Peterhead and as if, in fact, that was where she was. Beyond her I could see vaster, taller avenues of camellia, in a ravine running for almost half a mile towards the sea. A mimosa of late exceptional magnificence was being tossed about, like a tree of yellow foam, in the sea-wind, and every few moments a shower of shaken magnolia petals, a dozen saucers of camellias, killed by the weight of their own perfection, would be shaken down in a shudder of pink and white, so that everywhere the grass was covered with petals mingling with the pale yellow hillocks of rejected lovely weeds.

As we drove down from this garden,

overwhelmed by its casual splendours, its Englishness, its prodigal luxuriance, I thought once again of all that can be done in gardens if frost is not there. Now and then the taxi-driver, a small dark-eyed neat man of exceptional politeness even on that island of great courtesy, stopped to break for us a branch of mountain mimosa or to run back up the road for a stalk of blue agapanthus, a flower we endlessly admired. Through deeper ravines we descended in a few minutes from spring to summer and so to the sea. Wild arum lilies began again to grow thick in ditches; sparkling scarlet geraniums and here and there a tomato plant, scarlet too with fruit, clung to volcanic iron-gleaming rock. Golden tubes of bignonia floated along garden fences, and roses spilled splendidly from villa walls. A glorious species of climbing begonia, rich-rose, made hedges of great beauty on trellis work, and pale blue Morning Glory, in cool combination with a large straw-coloured mesembryanthemum, poured from waste places. Hibiscus, that had been of crimson and salmon and rose-apricot, like big single Indian roses, were now almost over, and in some gardens Señor Pimpkins, bare-footed, shag-clouded, gawping, was already hard at work with his universal weapon, settin' back, shearing the bushes down. Wistarias were beginning to obliterate with their heavy richness the entire façades of large houses and everywhere the landscape was a denial, a rich mockery, of the notion that if you have too much of a thing you fail, in time, to appreciate it, of our curious northern notion that only by struggling through the tomb of winter can you really appreciate spring, and of our special English fallacy that a touch of frost in the air, like damp rooms and early closing hours, is somehow good for the soul.

7 *Railway Flowers*

When I was a child we came southward in the summer time; we were part of a great surging exodus that came down, every August, to the sea; and whenever I woke from a doze of over-excitement in crowded and sulphury railway carriages somewhere about Sevenoaks it was to find myself in a region of telegraph poles dreamily striding like slow-motion dancers on black stilts against the sky and to be a little dazzled, in the moment of waking, by flashing gullies of white chalk and the bright gaiety of a world that has fascinated me ever since: the world of railway flowers.

There is no one, I imagine, who at some time or other has not wanted to pull a communication cord, stop a train, get out and with disregard of penalties and timetables wander off along those narrow sloping paradises of primroses in spring, moon daisies in high summer and foamy clematis seed in autumn that mark, everywhere in this country, the changing of the railway seasons. There are people who travel always by air because, as they say, it saves time. I have never known what you do with time when you save it and there will always remain with me a great fondness for the leisure of rail travel and more especially for little trains that peep and fuss away, as the tram-train from Morlaix to St Jean du Doigt in Brittany does or the cog-wheel from Lauterbrunnen to Scheidegg or the toy train across Romney marshes or even the casual locals that sidle through summery valleys of Welsh hay, into lost and flowering worlds of their own. Time saved is never so beautiful as time spent and almost all the hours I ever saved by flying now seem dreary beside those I wasted on little trains creeping up and down their private valleys of flower.

To these hours belong a miraculous

evening in April, in war-time, when one of these lethargic locals in which Oxfordshire specializes took me along twenty double miles of cowslips into a western sky steeped in cowslip-coloured light. You could put the windows of the carriage down at the little local station and the scent of a thousand cowslips, so tender and honied, would pour in. The whole evening sprang with gold. And in much the same way, a year later, along valleys coming out of Wales, the light of a July moon leapt out of mile after mile of moon-daisies, so many and so lush that they were quite fiery with whiteness.

Yet I can never decide if these special illuminations by one sort of flower are more enchanting than the common mixture that grows thicker and richer on railway cuttings as summer goes on. As blue-bell and prim-rose and violet give way to pink and white campion the whole milky richness of June is made lovelier by half-wild things that escape from gardens and colonize themselves. There is always a splendid cliff of the slenderest pink and mauve Canterbury bells on the chalk about Sevenoaks and another of red Valerian a mile or two away, and unless I am much mistaken there are a few grey grasses of garden pink there, springing from chalk fissures that hold, earlier, little gnarled and golden trees of wallflower. And from country stations everywhere there is always a wandering off, beyond the train limits of rambler-rose and lily and geranium and lobelia, of flag-iris and marigold and lupin and evening primrose into banks of broom and dog-rose. That same yellow evening primrose, fully wild, flaring against black miles of German pine-forest belongs, for me, to a whole world of garden flowers that turn out, on foreign railway tracks, to be nothing but the wildest weeds. Amber-brown day lilies and scarlet-yellow bignonia all along the tracks of Virginia in June; purple aquilegia and Christmas rose and Solomon's seal and cyclamen in Northern Italy; purple pasque-flower in France; and up any alpine railway of middle Europe the slow rise of lovelier and lovelier things, out of a rich world of meadow-salvia and lucerne into a world of mealy yellow primula and golden trollius and white narcissus and so up into the rare high world of tumbling winding ridges of crocus and gentian and soldanella and half-melted snow. Odd that out of hundreds of miles of travel India should have nothing, as far as I am concerned, to add to that: only a haunting recollection of dark women grovelling between blistering sleepers for their miserable crumbs of fallen coal and of service nurses coming back on leave from the north, carrying into the stupefying heat of Calcutta, cool baskets of common primrose gathered, very possibly, on the banks of that half-toy railway that takes you on the last stages of the journey to Darjeeling and the sight of great snows.

The same sort of aridity belongs to the narrow-gauge one-track line, cutting across the glare of flat white desert, described in *The Purple Plain*. Trainless, flowerless, treeless, that derelict track going out of nowhere into nothing, under harshly glittering sun, remains with me always in discomforting brightness, a depressing and in some way sinister symbol of Burma's ruin under war. Those who have never seen the East can have no possible conception of the melancholy and fatalistic tawdriness produced on the neglected works of man by the horror of constant sun; yet the little railway in Burma, empty and sunk in yellow dust, never fails to remind me of another nearer home. The little narrow-track railway, almost a toy, running along the Kentish coast between Hythe and Dymchurch and New Romney, always seems to me on the verge of disappearance into the half-shore of shingle across which it puffs and peeps its way with loads of Gulliver-like holiday-makers. Its landscape of yellow shingle, brightened by drifts of fox-glove and yellow sea-poppy, bright blue viper's-bugloss and marsh-mallow, floppy pink convolvulus and salt-blue sea-thistle, is unique in railway travel; and the little train itself belongs to the world that all travellers in little things adore and of which railway flowers are so precious a part.

I do not know if there will ever be, in a comparable way, in a future where Hurricanes and Blenheims and Flying Fortresses are regarded affectionately as being as antique as Puffing-Billy, any sort of history of air-way flowers. The only airfield I know that has any of the sea-shore charm of the miniature railway of Romney Marsh is the one at Nice, where in almost the same way great air-liners, after circling the bay, taxi in across a narrow shore of shingle, coming to rest on a dusty landscape of dune grass and bright pine-thatched huts selling *langouste* and *bouillabaisse*. But there ought to be, and probably already is, a history of roadside flowers, which in this cool slow year in England have been magnificent. The long wet winter produced, in May and early June, a splendour of common kex un-equalled through the season by any other flower. It ran with cloudy lacy glory all over the south, but its airy green-white grace, on deep and narrow roads, was merely nothing compared with its grandeur along the wide and clayey roads of the Midlands, and its richness there was as nothing again compared with the solid forest of it along the fen-roads of Lincoln and Cambridge and Huntingdonshire, where it towered to six feet or more, common and rampant and yet somehow always delicate and of infinite transparent grace, a lovely foretaste of the meadow-sweet and the modest codlins-and-cream that would replace it in July.

On a journey in and about the middle ribs of England and a little later through the lush forested parts of Hampshire and West Sussex, where a certain stuffy airlessness descends on the heavily-timbered landscape, we must have seen a thousand miles of it, if you count the roadside as a double strip. Whether it was more beautiful by day or by night it is hard to say. In my native Northamptonshire and again on the incomparable reaches of the Ouse about Paxton it had almost a greenish phosphorescence seen in the car head-lights in the first calm warm nights of early June. Through this intensely English countryside five of us drove with happy nostalgia, in and out of little villages of tawny and pink and green and yellow stucco, remembering our grandfathers and the days of neat black buggies and of journeys by rose-starred hedges in late Edwardian summer-times. My mother spoke of a holiday in a village shop, in a garden with a fig-tree and madonna lilies overlooked by modest Georgian windows, where the lodgings for four people came to thirty shillings; my wife remembered her frequent tears, on wet Sundays, when the rain would never end and the little black trap, costing ten shillings for the day, could not be hired from the local purveyor of flies and hearses and wagonettes. We remembered a life intensely localized, unexpanded beyond its familiar boundaries by the internal combustion engine and its revolution. We recalled, as we drove past them, great houses, and how in those days we had been cut off from them by seemingly inviolate class distinctions, as from the palaces of Mogul emperors; and we saw the houses, set in walled gardens stark with shattered hot-houses, now in decay. We remembered, as if we were doddering and toothless creatures of great age instead of people in our early forties, a life of apparently unambitious gentleness, of charm unsavaged by repeated war.

In this reminiscence about the swiftness of change and the harshness of distinctions it occurred to us all that our time had given us at least one special pleasure. In our youth, still more in our remote horse-bound childhood, there had been hardly any travelling by night. It is true that sometimes on feast-days we went off into what seemed to me an incredibly far-off foreign country. Dust and dew lay together on miles of pink briar roses; an abundance of meadow-sweet smothered lush roads by river meadows. I used to catch enchanting glimpses of lakes under the shadow of the same great houses we now saw in decay and of rivers of white water-lilies floating placidly away to even farther, stranger, deeper country that could never be explored. From these journeys we came back, sometimes, in summer darkness, and before we started home, or perhaps after we had started, the carriage lamps of the little trap would be lighted and would continue with us, in a moth-haunted, flower-ghost world, like jolly running flames.

Now when all of us travel on roads by night there are times when I think the progression by beamed white car light, through country lanes, in summer-time, has even greater enchantment than the night journeys of childhood by candle-flame. I am not at all sure it is not the greatest single joy of motoring. In the days of trap and horse you were as much a part of the world through which you travelled as the air blowing past you. You stretched up your hand and let it be brushed by leaves; you hung it over the trap-side and let it be washed by waves of grasses. Road and yourself and vehicle and lights were one; you went along together. It created the deepest essence of tranquillity, without surprise. Speed had not begun to bring to millions of us a sense of being hurled into tracks of fierce illumination populated by racing feathers of grass and flower, by astonished owl and rabbit, by snowfalls of bewildered moths rushing to death on windscreens. It had not yet begun to add to the mystery of night travelling a feeling of the tensest surprise and excitement, a sense of being projected over the edge of darkness, that must formerly have been known only to the drivers of night expresses.

The degree of this excitement and pleasure varies inversely, of course, to the size of the road. By-passes and autostrada – through the straight crazy kilometres of *Martini Rossi, Martini Rossi, Martini Rossi, Martini Rossi, Bel Paese, Bel Paese, Bel Paese,*

Bel Paese, flung at you like the boards of armies of super-sandwichmen, have their own appalling fascination – can never have the beauty of little roads, where the sickle is always a little slow in its attack on grass and daisy and kex, so that in early June nights the car lights seem to be pouring down on a world of lace, of mysteriously lovely creamy-green entanglements of flower from which night-moths are blown as if they were torn petals.

This first phase of early summer, when kex and grass and cow-parsley and campion and rose and daisy flaunt up in hedgerows to first full lush riot of flower, gives the most haunting loveliness to journeys on little roads by night. Much earlier, even before the end of winter, streaming pennants of hazel catkins dart out of woodland. Primroses wink unexpectedly from steep roadside banks. On chalk hills the first new leaves of whitebeam have the flaming purity of magnolia. The chalk itself has the beauty of running dead-white flame.

By April and May all the foamy ghosts of blackthorn and hawthorn go streaming past: to be reincarnated as it were, months later, in the ghostlier foam of traveller's joy. By the end of June darkening leaf has smothered all tree-flower. Small apple-green chestnuts hang in clustered sprays like pendant lanterns. Grasses grow gradually taller and whiter, more corn-like, more dusty; the car is sprayed with seed. A new phase begins, the loveliest of all: the stars of countless moon-daisies; spikes of meadow-sweet shot with poppy, a fluffy splendour of cream and scarlet racing out of the darkness; and then mistier, softer, more dissolving, masses of mauve scabious and wild marjoram and willow-herb, all individual colour bleached out of them by light. Now, if you drive with windows open or in open cars, scent streams in: that almost too exotic night-odour of honeysuckle and hay and first tobacco plant staring over the fences of cottage gardens. The later at night you travel, in summer especially, the more heady and mysterious and fascinating it grows. Not only flowers and trees and grasses now: but people. Odd lights in dark villages, stray lovers saying good-night, bicycles snaking shakily down remote lanes, ducking figures in parked cars, policemen waiting at scarlet phone-boxes: who are they? what are their lives? what goes on? Headlights pour with the merciless ferocity of searchlights telescoping on worlds unexplored, dramas the novelist longs to unravel, to play with and piece together again. There is a gasp at the beauty of rose-covered walls streaming past in the dead of night that recalls earlier beauties already for-gotten: whole orchards of cherry and apple folding and unfolding in spring darkness.

Towards the end of the war I used to drive, every day and almost every night, out of the heart of Calcutta to the perimeter of native suburbs up the Hooghli. It is perhaps the most repellent slum journey in the world. Towards the end of it there was a little street that cut through native huts between the crumbling stucco walls of two great houses.

Scarlet hibiscus and purple-salmon bougainvillaeas flamed in the lights of the jeep; over the garden walls there would be a vivid tender flash of dusty banana leaves and the scarlet claws of a silk cotton. The last mile to the Hooghli began by an opium shop. In a few seconds the dusty, deserted floweriness of the little short-cut was gone. Jeep lights poured down on streets of sleeping Indian figures. A face or two turned and hid itself with dark hands from the brilliance of light; dark feet curled and stirred. The rows of charpoys had a curiously stunted bludgeoned look; the white dhotis lying on them, in doorways, on pavements and in gutters, had the look of shrouds. The fierce white headlights swept over them as prison searchlights sweep over restless prisoners planning to escape in American jail films, leaving the exhausted and anonymous bodies just as securely imprisoned, and to all intents and purposes just as doomed.

Today I hardly ever travel through English summer lanes, by night, without thinking of it. The haunting, fascinating ugliness of one world heightens and deepens the beauty of the other. As summer goes on and the heat rises and corn ripens there has only to be in the air, for one moment, the faintest breath of heat or fire before the bougainvilleas, the hibiscus, the scarlet silk cottons and the rows and rows of abandoned bodies, undisturbed even by the march of cockroaches as large as mice, are flashing at me out of tropical darkness: to make me glad, for the thousandth time, that I need know nothing more medieval than a church spire, that I can go home and swing the car lights between the tubs of scarlet and white geraniums, to startle the last rabbits into the grass and perhaps a white owl beating low like a trailed shroud itself over my village common. And to be gladdened above all, as well as exhilarated and enriched, by the spectacular and yet private beauty of a night-world, full of lighted ghosts, that only we of our century know.

8 *The Show*

July comes in with days of high-feathered cloud and hot distances and the sound of hay-mowers down the valley. The trees give shade that is black under straight noon sun. Sometimes in the still morning heat there is hardly a sound except the crack of snails being broken by thrushes on paths, and then perhaps the drone of a watching pigeon, hidden somewhere among the cypresses as he contemplates the fattening peas below. All bird sound has become desultory, sometimes scrambled, and none of it, except the occasional trill of a wren or a yellowhammer, can now be called a song. There is a certain irritation about the grating, half-laughing voices of jackdaws. The nesting season has gone on very late and now, in the thickened garden, it is a common thing to see fat pairs of bewildered shining eyes staring up from odd corners: squabby, new-fledged thrushes, squatting like yellow-brown frogs, lost and waiting to be rescued and fed. On the pergola a pair of chaffinches, following the tradition of twenty years, have built late among the scarlet climbers, and soon too the young chaffinches flop from the nest a little before their time, fuzzy and almost the colour of summer-browned grass, and skulk help-lessly under flowers, while their parents twitter fussily above. Somehow, at night, they are gathered up, only to get hopelessly astray and dispersed again next day. A few days earlier a family of blue-tits took the air, but they were more ordered, a real tight little family squadron, always in close formation, never moving without each other. Where the parents led they followed, with a leap-frog of flight, clamouring not to be left behind, always grizzling to be fed. Even now, full grown, they never leave each other but are always dashing about the garden in an excited string, one of those inseparable families that always hang together.

These are perhaps the last of the summer's nests, though there will always be a thrush or a wren that builds later still, and the only other family man at the moment is the fly-catcher. He has taken up his post, as I write, on a stake in the dahlia border, and his method is rather like that of a fisherman fishing a favourite stretch of stream. From his post he watches with remarkable still-ness and patience, sometimes for minutes together, and then suddenly he darts down with a spinning leaf-like flight that ends in a curious snap at the air. In a second he is back on his post again, always the same post, though there are others he could use as well, and then he is off again, making always his clicking snap at the fly in mid-air, neat and sure and smart as the snapping of minute fingers. This goes on for about an hour, in which time I get so used to him watching and snapping and spinning and departing and always coming back to the same post in the same way that I am suddenly astonished to see him return and sit as it were side-saddle half-way up the post, his feathers now all brilliant crimson and gold, as if he had really rushed off and done a remarkable quick-change act out of sight. It is some moments before I realize that a gold-finch has arrived instead, to be joined almost immediately by his fussy affectionate mate, who prances round with child-like excitement for a moment before dragging him away. But before they go they are framed for one moment against a background of gold and crimson aquilegias, almost exactly their own colour and with much of their own prancing delicacy as they quiver in the morning wind.

A few days of heat have brought the garden, the countryside and the summer to the height of their beauty. Just as W. H. Hudson used to say that spring in England reached its perfection on or about May the 18th, at the time of oak-flower and may-blossom and chestnut and nightingale, so it is almost infallible for summer to reach its high perfection on or about July the 7th, at the time of rose and lily and black oak-shade and the fusion of hay and corn. Between that date and somewhere about the twentieth of the month the corn is most beautiful; there is a baffling loveliness in the colour of wheat in the weeks immediately before its turning. A sort of blueness, touched with grey, rather like the colour of a carnation leaf, gives it in the first days of July a delicate bloom; but even then it is already changing, to become as the days go past more and more olive, a few shades lighter, and then still more lucent, until in its time of pre-ripeness, past the blue, past green, past gold, it has all the light of a summer sea. In the new ranges of wheat hybrids there is now one that, in the weeks of midsummer, is of a curious blue-whiteness, remarkably light and shining, and there is a barley, perhaps not new, of which all the bristles are very pink and very long, like exceptionally fancy moustaches. There are not many oats this year, perhaps because of an autumn that made corn sowing almost impossible, and I shall miss the pink-gold of them, in the first days of cutting, and then the shining deep butter yellow of the full ripe straw.

There begins, about now, the rather fearsome but not unlikeable business of flower shows. The curious mentalities of the Mr Pimpkinses have a new world in which to exercise themselves. For it is at all times very noticeable that the Mr Pimpkinses and Mr Dolittles are not only men of curious habit and dark suspicion; they are convinced that queer forces of persecution are for ever at work against them. In the early weeks of June you begin to inquire, for example, and with perfectly reasonable friendliness, what produce Mr Pimpkins will be exhibiting at the Show, which takes place in late July, a good month ahead, at a time which seems to you admirably chosen to catch all the richness and beauty of the gardening year. To your astonishment Mr Pimpkins lets out such a belching sneer of scorn, first about the date of the flower show, then about the despicable practice of flower shows in general, then about certain deep and unnamable subversive forces at work for their own selfish ends behind the scenes of flower shows, that you are quite sorry you ever brought the matter up.

'Show?' Mr Pimpkins says, and he manages to infuse into the word all the vinegary and miserable disgust usually reserved for words like rat, blackmail, quisling and so on, 'Tah! Show? Call it a show? What show? Like the one they 'ad last year?' and he gives a sort of grizzly, bony 'Tckl! Tckl! Tckl!' of altogether horrible scorn, champing his moustaches.

The fierce and unreasonable tone of all this is both baffling and depressing. In your view the show last year was, in a modest way, excellent; it was one of those pleasant communal country affairs in which people displayed the fruits of their labours with pride and pleasure and where nothing was taken with that deadly competitive seriousness that so often introduces a canker of jealousy into the whole proceedings. True, the gawping hangers-back were, as always, there: waiting to see which way the cat jumped, reluctant to be part of a failure and yet longing for a failure to be born. They did not, however, infect the affair too greatly and it succeeded, you thought, in spite of them.

'I thought it wasn't bad,' you say.

'Some done all right,' Mr Pimpkins says. 'Some done all right out on it.'

You do not know quite what Mr Pimpkins means by some done all right out on it but you guess, knowing Mr Pimpkins, that he is on the verge of charging unnamed persons with deceit, perhaps with sharp practice, perhaps even with downright dishonesty.

'I coulda told you who wur goon git the prizes afore it started,' Mr Pimpkins says. 'I knowed all right. I coulda told you.'

'Really?'

'Allus the same click,' Mr Pimpkins says. 'Allus 'as bin. Allus will be.' He then utters the dark and withering word 'committee.'

From all this you gather that Mr Pimpkins is utterly convinced the flower show is rigged; that all flower shows are run by and for a privileged and miserable few; and that he, for one, will have no part of them.

'So you won't be showing?' you say.

'Puzzle me to,' Mr Pimpkins says. 'Bout all I've got is a few titty little taters, that's all.'

'What about peas?' For weeks Mr Pimpkins has been driving you frenzied by comparing your pods of *Laxton's Superb*, which you yourself think are excellent, with his own superb specimens of a particularly stupendous giant variety, a world-beater, of which he is careful not to tell you the name.

'Jays evvin 'em,' Mr Pimpkins says. 'Strippin' 'em orf fast as they come. Shan't ev a pea.'

You say something about birds being terrible things and Mr Pimpkins says:

'Ent got no carrots, neether. Yit no onions.'

You are about to ask after beans, which in other years Mr Pimpkins grows by his own secret process to a length of thirty inches or so, probably by hanging weights on the end of them, when Mr Pimpkins anticipates you:

'Shent ev a pea. Shent ev a bean. Shent ev nothing, what I can see on it.'

'Oh! dear.'

'You goon show?'

It had been your intention to exhibit, perhaps, a few modest bowls of flowers, a pot or two of your prized begonias and, almost certainly, something from the rose-garden, your pride and joy.

'Must put in a few roses,' you say.

'Got the fly summat chronic, ent they?' Mr Pimpkins says.

Fly, you admit, has been rather trying; but–

'Smothered with black-spot, an' all, ent they?'

Black-spot, too, has been bad. However–

'Et ev 'em all out in th' autumn, I reckon,

wunt y'?' Mr Pimpkins says. 'Start afresh?'

As you have between four and five hundred rose-trees and as you have no intention whatsoever of uprooting them for Mr Pimpkins or anybody else or for all the fly and black-spot in the world, this is the end of all immediate conversation on the subject of flower shows. You begin to retire, affronted. But Mr Pimpkins, departing at the same moment with dreary glances at our inadequate Laxton's Superb, has the final word:

'Prizes ent big enough. Ent wuth the trouble gittin' stuff up. Still, if you ent got it, you ent got it, so there y'are.'

So there you are. Mr Pimpkins, pessimist, belly-acher, altogether a horror of misery, with neither pea nor bean to his name, puts his blight on flower shows and all they stand for. If you ent got it, as he so rightly says, you ent got it. And there you are.

Soon, in a week or two, the morning of the flower show arrives. You get up reasonably early with the amiable intention of getting the vegetable part of your exhibits ready before breakfast. You have decided to show half a dozen of what Mr Pimpkins always calls 'kitney taters,' a dozen pods of peas and a plate of Bedfordshire Champion onions, Mr Pimpkins does not grow Bedfordshire Champion; he grows a variety known, in his language, as 'Triplohs,' a large red Tripolitanian winter onion growing as large as a football. Since Mr Pimpkins has, however, in the season of his famine, neither onions nor carrots, indeed nothing at all, you feel encouraged to exhibit your own onions, which are about as large as decent sized paper weights and not at all unattractive.

You begin by digging the potatoes. The first three roots yield one potato of tolerable shape as against something like fifty of what are known as chats. Previously your potatoes have yielded splendid specimens of even shape, almost too large for cooking. You dig again. This time you unearth the most astonishing variety of potato shapes, from cottage loaves to noses of fantastic bulbousness, together with two potatoes of perfect shape, one of which you promptly spear with your fork. You dig again. In three hills, as they are called in the south country, you cannot discover a single potato that has not a scar, scab, slug-hole, blight-patch, worm-bore, deformity or defect of some kind. You have now dug, it seems, half a bushel of potatoes and your reward is two potatoes of possible shape and size. You dig again. This time you are confronted with an entirely new situation. Whereas you had begun to select potatoes of a certain slenderness, of the true kidney pattern, you are now suddenly presented with three perfect potatoes whose common characteristic is a certain roundness, combined with an attractive flatness and an admirable smoothness of skin. You decide to discard, now, the first potatoes and to concentrate on the finding of three more to match the second. But the next root yields, as potatoes sometimes will, only one potato, of prodigious size and almost perfect shape, weighing about a pound. You are so intent on admiring this that in your preoccupation you turn sharply and step on the finest of the rounded triplets, crushing it in half. You dig again. At the same time you realize, with annoyance and some horror, that you have now dug no less than a third of the entire new potato crop and that if things continue in this way you will undoubtedly dig the lot. In despair you make an unhappy rush at the whole problem, select six potatoes that have no possible chance of fooling anybody and go to breakfast.

After breakfast you turn to peas. To select twelve pea pods of even size and colour would appear to be the simplest thing in the world next to shelling them. There is, in fact, no more tiresome gardening problem. Pea pods can assume, it appears, even more shapes than potatoes; some are hooked, some are twisted, some have become bent and scarred; birds have played havoc among them; most of them are pock-marked. They are either too flat, a fortnight early, or too plump, a fortnight late. But in due course, anyway, the peas are chosen and they are not, perhaps, too intolerable after all. The onions, on the contrary, are a tragedy. To your horror your wife, or the cook, or one of the children perhaps, has calmly selected those of the largest size and made off with them to the kitchen; these were the onions, undoubtedly, that smothered your minute portion of steak at supper last night; and sadly, irately, you realize that you cannot have your onions and eat them too.

With some relief you turn to flowers. Here, you feel, you will be on easier, simpler ground. Fondly you imagine that it is simply a question of a few minutes with the secateurs. You begin, accordingly, with the roses. Twenty minutes later you are faced with the horrifying truth that on several hundred bushes there are exactly three possible roses of exhibition quality. An hour later you have discovered two forgotten and rather mildewed specimens on the house wall and you are searching with some desperation for the sixth when your wife calls from the house that it is now eleven o'clock and weren't the exhibits supposed to be staged by half past ten? You cannot remember. You have still the lilies to cut, the Vase or Basket of Flowers Arranged for Effect to do, the specimen pots of begonias to find. You begin suddenly to feel hot, panicked and rather tired. Then you discover that the begonias, in their maddening way, have dropped their flowers in the night and that your exquisite specimens lie ruined, like flabby orange and scarlet rosettes, on the greenhouse floor. The morning's only consolation is in the lilies. They at least, with their stately marbled heads, their cool white perfection, are incomparable. No one could possibly compete with them; it is doubtful, indeed, if any other competitor will ever have heard of such exclusive Regale hybrids, for which you paid fabulous prices in the spring.

In due course you leave the house in

unpleasant haste with your few wretched vegetables and your flowers. As you are packing them into the car you see the younger Miss Bossingham go by. You do not like the younger Miss Bossingham and for some reason Miss Bossingham, perhaps not unnaturally, does not like you. Miss Bossingham, who has something of the appearance of an infertile and moulting hawk, lives with her invalid sister, a matriarch of formidable temperament who broods savagely in a bath chair, convinced that there ought to be no such things as neighbours, a philosophy with which, after many dreary years of living next door to her, you are inclined to agree. In the course of many years you have received solicitors' letters from the Miss Bossinghams on every kind of subject, from the necessity of controlling dogs, which anyway you do not keep, to the question of babies' napkins obscuring the view, at two hundred yards' distance, from the Bossingham conservatory. At one time or another the Miss

Bossinghams have kept terriers, Alsatians, parrots, budgerigars, Siamese cats, goats and guinea fowl. They have a brother, Charlie Bossingham, a short-sighted gentleman who comes down to see them once a year and who on one occasion mistook your house for theirs, walked in, called you Edna, the name of the elder Miss Bossingham, and wondered how you came to be doing so well without the bath chair. In every village in the world there are, I suppose, Miss Bossinghams; but England, above all, is their spiritual home. Like wet summers, thin bread and butter, licensing hours and cricket, they are deep-rooted in our pattern.

This morning, as Miss Bossingham goes past, driving her pre-war Ford and smoking as usual her shabby cigarette, with an Alsatian as large as a calf sitting on the seat beside her, you observe that the car is full of flowers. Magnificent flowers. There are also vegetables. Magnificent vegetables. You stare, but Miss Bossingham does not see you. She looks through, past, about and over you with a horrible sort of triumph; and then vanishes, through a gnashing of gears, with her load of flowers. You follow her to the village hall.

There, to your infinite astonishment, is Mr Pimpkins. Mr Pimpkins is just putting the finishing touches to a dish of 'triplohs.' These onions are gross, brilliantly impossible vulgar; they shine like satin and have stems, fancily tied with raffia, like stalks of bloated cow parsley. You have never seen such onions, a man could live for months on one of them. The onions being finished, Mr Pimpkins is presently heard calling 'Moind y' backs' and now appears with a large green tray, which you realize is Class B, Section 45, Tray or Box of Vegetables, not less than 8 varieties, Box not to exceed 2 ft. 6 in. by 3 ft. 6 in., all vegetables to be grown by the exhibitor. Mr Pimpkins staggers in with this monstrous affair, on which there is a prodigal and succulent arrangement of broad beans, cos and cabbage lettuce, gigantic peas, twinkling radishes, kitney and round potatoes and young cauliflowers, all resting on a curly and vivid bed of parsley. The iniquitous treachery of it all leaves you speechless. You retire, flustered and hot, to arrange your roses. Two minutes later Mr Pimpkins, who to your knowledge has only six rose trees that grow in a dreary plot between a cycle shed and a water barrel, appears with an exhibit of roses of quite exceptional splendour: of long stems and blooms exquisitely pointed, of petals curled as if with brushes of camel hair and curling tongs. You retreat, livid and wretched, to the table reserved for lilies. To your relief Mr Pimpkins does not follow you there. You are confronted instead by Miss Bossingham, in khaki slacks, cigarette dangling, altogether as unfeminine and repugnant as can be, who is arranging a four-foot vase of *Lilium Croceum* with a certain air of controlled savagery. The air about her is tense. Miss Bossingham has never spoken to you since the lamentable affair of the cesspool and there has been no communication between you whatsoever since your icy rejection, a masterpiece as it seemed to you of clinical and killing irony, of her suggestion that you should not hang your washing on the line. Now, silent in tense and deadly enmity, you stand side by side, not a foot separating you, she with her savage orange beauties, you with your white marbled trumpets dustily golden. It is typical, of course, of the habit of *Lilium Regale* with its heavy-headed stalks, that nothing on earth will make it stand up properly in the vase; whereas Miss Bossingham's erect and upstanding *croceums* do so with superb ease, as if they were growing there. In the middle of all this, Miss Bossingham breaks the tension with a giggle, sloppy, almost a little hysterical, queerly forced, as it seems almost for a moment as if she is going to speak to you; but nothing happens, and in a moment Miss Bossingham, flushed and frustrated, haughtily takes herself away.

Fortunately it is not merely Miss

Bossingham and Mr Pimpkins who are there. The little village hall, now so sweet and gay with flowers, so soundly fragrant with summer scent and the smell of earth, is full of people who are very English, very friendly, on the whole, very pleasant. They have been brought together, most of them, not by notions of competition, but by a common affection for gardens, and the things, material and spiritual, that gardens give. The president, an amiable, cultured, rather plump gentleman of friendly character, is there; Mr Browning, of the cricket club, living a life devoted otherwise to the raising of tomatoes, is there; the coal merchant is arranging his sweet-peas and the carpenter is breathing reverently over his carnations; Harry, the horse-keeper with the cheeky blue eyes and the manner of a droll puppet, who seems normally interested in nothing but the pint, the pin-table and the dart-board, has an almost religious air about him as he curls the last quill of his pink and orange and scarlet dahlias. Little girls arrive with jam-pots of wild flower, pretty mixtures of meadow-sweet and poppy and wild-rose and scabious, and small boys with jam-pots full of cabbage butterflies. The rather garrulous Miss de Bere enters with sections of comb honey and a seed-cake. Even the parson arrives.

At twelve o'clock the president's wife arrives with the judges and in the little hall there is a sudden scuffling among the lettuces and onions, a desperate last minute arrival of old ladies with salads and plum cakes. This possibly accounts for the fact that many people get their exhibits wrongly staged, displaying six potatoes instead of five, or nine kinds of vegetables instead of eight. But in five minutes the judges are locked in and a hush comes down on the village while people go home to have their dinners. You yourself go home with the rather depressed feeling that everybody's exhibits are better than your own and that you will be lucky if you gain a second and third out of twelve entries. The morning's sunshine has in the meantime done wonderful things to the remaining roses, so that whereas there were not more than seven from which to choose at breakfast time there are now, maddeningly, at least a dozen of the loveliest quality.

At half past two you go back to the hall. A certain fine air of tension hangs about the entrance. Miss Bossingham is there. Mr Pimpkins, in solid church-like blue serge, with celluloid collar and clip-on necktie, is talking to the parson, who looks rather less like a primitive wood carving under a black saucer hat than usual. Miss de Bere is wearing a large cake-like hat decorated, most unsuitably for her age, with forget-me-nots. Old Mrs Parkhurst, who is splay-footed and wears old-fashioned box-calf boots that come half-way up her legs, comes crunching along, prodding forward with her umbrella. The treasurer of the cricket club, Mr Beaver, a youngish married man of friendly temperament who will later get very excited on his fifth or sixth glass of beer, is selling raffle tickets for an eight-weeks-old pig, a blue and white animal at present asleep in a wire cage. The president's gardener is selling tickets for two live goslings, a bottle of Australian sherry, a plucked chicken, a dozen eggs and a tin of treacle. Children are arriving by the score in perambulators, over the edges of which they peer like bright-eyed fledgling birds at their elders, the motor-cars and the little line of red, blue and yellow flags stretched across the village street.

After everyone had said how lucky we are that it has kept fine for us after all the weather we've been having you go into the hall. You do so with the most casual off-hand air. In reality you are tense: perhaps even trembling. Just inside the door you are waylaid by Mrs Armitage, the bailiff's wife, who wants you to guess how many beans there are in a jar. This delays you nearly five minutes, so that by the time you are free the array of sweet-peas, roses, perennials, Baskets of Flowers for Effect, dahlias and gladioli seem to dance confusedly before your eyes. But when at last you can see straight you receive the first of several surprises. Your perennials, which you thought were most ordinary, have won first prize; your lilies have beaten Miss Bossingham; your Basket of Flowers for Effect, scrambled up at the last moment, has won a second. Above all, your roses, though only second, have beaten Mr Pimpkins'. On the other hand your dahlias, which you thought splendid and in such good taste, have been cast aside in favour of some coarse vulgarities by the secretary of the Pig Club. Your vase for table decoration, an affair of miniature salmon gladioli and silver *cineraria maritima,* a piece of real artistry over which you spent hours, has been quite rejected; the prize in that section goes to an incredible jumble of orange helenium, rambler roses and gypsophila. You are trying to understand the workings of judges' minds when your friend Mr Finch arrives. Mr Finch, a dry, carefree, most genial man who does not know a carnation from a sweet-pea but is nevertheless fascinated by the mystery of horticulture, is a tireless joker. With solemnity he invites you to admire his *erysipelas procumbius*, begs you to take a look at his *amnesia forsythiensis*. And his *arthritis grandiflora*, he says, they are rather nice too, aren't they? It was his intention also to exhibit a few *sciatica lactiflora*, but they were ruined by a late attack of slug, leaving him only a few *eczema contagiensis* to bring along instead. Under these pleasantries your tension subsides. You proceed to tour the hall, and then the vegetable tent, in company with Mr Finch, who is tireless in conjuring his medical-botanical nonsense and equally tireless in his admiration for those who know, and can grow, the real thing. You pause together before sweet-peas whose leaves are like cabbages; before Mr Pimpkins' stunning array of vegetables. The tent glows with beetroot, silky pink onions, starry bunches of orange carrots, tomatoes and strawberries, black currants that are like grapes, and above all with healthy country faces reddened to fieriness by weeks in hay-fields. How English, how simple, how earthly and how eternal it suddenly seems. A young ex-Italian prisoner walks through the tent with his beautiful English wife and you cannot help wondering if such a situation would ever have been possible for a captured English boy after the defeat of his country; and as you ponder for a moment on the ruthlessness of the English in conflict and at the breadth of their magnanimity in peace you wonder if perhaps the root of it all is not here in the tent, lurking in the charm of the flower show, where in the morning there was a certain unpleasant sharp edge of competition in the air and where now, in the afternoon, there is peace and friendliness and a certain jocular resignation among the defeated, so well exemplified by Mr Finch, who bites his nails and sulkily says he will never exhibit again because his *thrombosis excelsis magnifica,* his favourite flower, has not received a prize.

Out of this pleasant, sleepy fragrant atmosphere, flushed by a modest sense of victory, you emerge to have tea. It is possible to take tea under the apple-trees, in an arbour of grass and pink pillar-roses and ramping elderberry, at the village pub. Trestle tables are set out in the shade. In the meadows on all sides hay is being cut and turned, filling the air with its fresh and floating sweetness, warm from July sun. In the pub paddock Mr Pettigrove's Flying Derby Winners, painted pale yellow and scarlet, together with a skittle alley and a few yellow swing-boats, make up a little fair. Children are beginning to run races. Young ladies begin to run races. There is shrieking and laughter in the air and soon Lizzie brings tomato sandwiches to the tables, with fresh-made tea. Mrs Parkhurst squeaks into the garden with her box-calf boots and sits munching toothlessly in the sun. A delicious tenderness of Old White cluster roses overpowers for a moment even the deep fragrance of hay, and suddenly you no longer wonder about England, its charm, its indefinable delight, the profound permanence of its habits and its beauty. Here it is, distilled. All your Englishness rises to the surface of your mind and your emotions in a moment of simple exultant pride in your country and in this special moment of country life, appealing so pleasantly to the heart, the eye and the senses, that cannot decay.

By the time you get back to the hall people are beginning to dismantle and take away their prize patterns of vegetables and baskets of flowers; everywhere lies the litter of a party that is almost over. Then for half an hour the president, aided by a number of rubicund gentlemen of the committee, auctions off, in an atmosphere of increasing jollity, those things that exhibitors do not wish to take away. Except that the proceedings are a little marred by the local bore, who cannot allow the circumstance of a pound of peas being sold without the heaviest facetiousness and who runs up the prices of baby vegetable marrows as if they were diamonds in order to show what a fine fellow he is, everything goes off very well and very heartily. The flowers have lost their freshness, but nobody seems to care; the fattest vegetables no longer seem quite so portentous; petals and lettuce leaves litter the hall and the path outside. Among all the exhibitors only Miss Bossingham, Mr Pimpkins and the high priests of the sweet-pea creed do not offer their produce for sale. The village street ripples with laughter in the evening sun. All acrimony has gone. And though you know perfectly well that the after-taste of it will be belched up, chewed on and regurgitated over many a pint of brown, on many an evening, in the bar of the pub, such narrow trivialities do not matter now. Perhaps Mr Beaver's peas were better than Mr Pimpkins' peas; perhaps Mr Armitage was grossly treated in the matter of his carnations. But you know that really, in their hearts, neither Mr Beaver nor Mr Armitage will care. You know that Mr Pimpkins, who was inexplicably beaten on broad beans by Miss Fawcett, a spinster, will care; and that Mr Beaver, over his fifth pint, will call him a silly old basket. You know that Mr Billings will nurse for a year a slight grievance that his superb alstromeria, in shades of pink, were awarded nothing whatever in the lily section, and that no amount of expert explanation of the fact that alstromerias are not lilies will ever quite console him in defeat. Old ladies begin to toddle home with their prize cakes, which they will eat, spiced up with a word or two, for Sunday tea. Children begin to grizzle in their prams. The local beauties begin to slip away in order to dress up for evening dancing. Miss Fawcett presently pipes up to thank the president, the president's wife and the members of the committee for 'their tireless efforts of behalf of…' the rest of her words lost in a dry flapping of applause. Arthur, the cowman, says to Mr Beaver that he 'reckons it's 'bout toime to goon ev one' and Mr Beaver, thirsty as ever, is not slow to agree. Sam Parks, a most cheerful man, who has eight children, staggers away with half a hundredweight of onions, carrots, turnips and potatoes, and Mrs Parks, grinning, follows with five of the children and what appears undoubtedly to be number nine. Little boys clutch their jam-jars of white butterflies, not knowing quite what to do with them and looking a little as if they are sorry for capturing them after all, and little girls go home with their sewing and their buttonholes. Everyone says what a wonderful show it has been, perhaps the best ever, and how lucky we were with the weather, and over everything there is a softening fragrance of May. The president thanks everyone for their support and appeals, in the last moment, for volunteers to sweep and straighten up the hall before the dance begins; but suddenly everyone, as always, in the most miraculous way, has something else to do.

The street empties itself. The grizzling

sleepy-dusted nestlings are taken home in their prams. You too go home, through meadows of drying hay and wild rose and late elder-flower, tired out but incomparably content, determined next year to beat everyone on roses and perhaps even Mr Pimpkins, just to show the old rascal, on onions and taters.

9 *All Summer in a Day*

On a day of delicate blue sky, with haze of pale smoky brown obscuring the distances over a skin-smooth sea, we take a small aeroplane from the landward cliff that is Lympne, from which you can see the entire half-circular basin of Romney Marsh below, and in twenty minutes we are through the curtains of haze, over glittering sandy muscles of shore, and then in France again.

Below us, in the last mile or two of England, a few hay-fields, in which the hay is cut but not carried, have the appearance of ancient mazes, of neat defensive earthworks made of low brown walls with straggling green moats of water between. A few toy ships are gliding up towards the misty cheese-like cliffs of Dover. For a few minutes Kent lies behind these cliffs like a piece of green, much-fissured crust of mould on the cheese, and then dissolves away. It seems really to melt, on this hot and beautiful morning, into nothing, off the face of earth. For some time we are between the two countries, neither visible, the sea below us made up of a series of calm blue islands, separated by still calmer bays and estuaries and ponds, the surface of each one like the skin of a limp bladder. It seems quite possible, during this short time, that we are lost, that France, like England, has melted off the earth; there is nothing to tell that a country lies to the north, and another to the south, only ten minutes away. Two hearty gentlemen in the aircraft, silk-shirted, already boisterous, free of their wives, are bound for France with something of the forced exuberance of prisoners released on parole. There is nothing at all in their friendly nosiness to suggest that they have ever thought, for one moment, that France might not be there, that some curious miracle of summer dissolution, some atomic

Atlantis-like trick, might have removed it from the earth. It is clear that they regard France as the land of wine, mid-summer dissipation and the free; and that they are going to bring to her, for the day, all the bountiful affection of their stifled English hearts. The thought crosses my mind for a moment of how trustful they and all of us are: childlike in our belief that because a diagrammatic pattern in blue and green and pink and yellow, a map, tells us that France or England or India or Italy are at this latitude and that longitude, we accept it in unshaken innocence without ever going out to see for ourselves, in boats or aircraft, with sextant and compass, whether it might or might not be true. But the thought is no sooner there than gone, and no sooner gone than France does appear, climbing out of the summer haze like a piece of more solid cloud, at first pale yellow, then greenish, and then, in a succession of brighter and clearer contours of coastline, white and green-blue and brown.

Here, where the river flows up the wide estuary past the orange-red houses of Etaples, the pattern of sands is fascinating. The sand bar at the river mouth, like an enormous basking arrowheaded shark, is already dry in places, almost bleached from morning sun. Underwater contours fade from fawn to smudgy green and then to purer green and blue. A few children are running across the sands, making feather-footed patterns that are simply light scribbles among the darker tracks of cars. The estuary, and also the outer sea, is dotted with sailless fishing boats. Great dry sugar-sandy dunes, graced with gorse and pines, lie behind the shore in unpopulated folds across which a track runs down emptily to an empty bay. Then the aircraft is over the marsh-like tongue of land separating the estuary from open sea: a long fin of indentured crust, moss-like, broken at regular intervals by saucer-like clearings that might have been, and perhaps still are, the means of gathering salt. As we go lower and lower the lichen-like crust becomes thicker, more cushiony, until it is a whole series of bumpy islands intersected by sandy veins through which high tides come creeping and running in; and then there is a sudden merging of island into one flat lump of mossiness and in turn into grass and bushes and yellow rag-wort and bleaching swathes of hay. And so, with whoopings of delight from the silk-shirted Englishmen who for one day are free of their country's curious and many puritanisms, not the least of which as far as they are concerned is a reluctance to recognize the fact that a man may get thirsty at hours unprescribed by law, we touch down on French soil. Gone, for one day, are the petty legacies of war, the niggling regimentations, the orderliness, the parochial, too-English memories of flower shows: the life beyond the Channel.

At once I am aware of an air of pleasant and growing carelessness. The silk-shirted gentlemen feel it too and rush off, waving passports, to take the first refreshment of the day under brilliant emerald and scarlet sunshades. We begin walking, and the sun is hot on the grey sandy path of forest. Under the shade of birch-trees and hornbeams the soil is still dark with rain but everywhere outside, in gardens, in park-like spaces at the entry to the town, the European passion for grass-watering is in full spate. Everything is being drenched from the nozzles of powerful hoses and the air is consequently full of the delicious odours of dust laid by rain. Through the forest, the streets and the gardens goes a continuous procession of young women whom Boudin's crinolined ladies, painted under the high white clouds of this northern coast seventy or eighty years ago, could only have looked upon as completely naked. Petal-like triangles reveal, rather than conceal, the shapes of countless bosoms; delicate trousers, short, neat, in brown and cerise and sailor shades of blue, reveal legs in infinite gradations of plumpness and slenderness. Down on the wide hot shore even these things are discarded. Yet apart from them there is hardly anything to tell that this is not, as it was in the 'seventies and 'eighties, Boudin's scene: the same pellucid lofty sky, the same combing white waves, the same umbrellas, the same red-and-white striped tents housing, over sleepy knitting, the same mamas and grandmamas gossiping while children play. Two wars do not seem to have touched it. The presence of a great number of very French, very matriarchal, very shrewd gran'mères, taking the long sea-side holiday with their grandchildren, all so much in the French tradition, is the thing, perhaps above all others, that helps to tie the scene down to the past and indeed to all time, making it eternal.

In this scene, under a dazzling July heat, facing the smallest bristling sea-breeze that burns every bit as sharply as the sun, we doze through an afternoon made pleasantly noisy by hordes of small French children disporting themselves in what, on large scarlet and white banners, is called a

Concours de Fromage. The French, who used to be considered a rather languid and unsporting race, despising the English passion for muscular achievements out of doors, are now passionately devoted to such things. Everywhere, on French beaches, in summer-time, there are always concours de something or other in progress at which benevolent manufacturers of cheese or sausage or mustard or motor tyres give away balloons or windmills to fat butter-brown infants running races on the sands. When evening comes the races are still going on, the gran'mères are still knitting with impervious matriarchal calm, the young ladies are still undressing and dressing in the Arab-like striped tents in full view of everybody, and the Frenchness of the scene intensifies in the calm blue air and the sunlight that seems still to bristle hotly across the dunes. And then, leaving all this to find a place to eat, we come across one of those funereal and at the same time loquacious waiters who are always glad to

242

talk on the startling and incredible decadence that has overtaken England: a circumstance on which his very first comment is a revelation.

It is brought about by the fact that we order wine. Most Englishmen, it seems, order beer; most Americans either milk or water; and both of them grumble incessantly over the quality of the French versions of their national beverages. The waiter has a long, dark-fissured, melancholy face that would look better on a miserable celibate priest or a jailer or someone of similarly circumscribed outlook, though it is also, undoubtedly, a common and universal face among waiters. The fact that we want to eat meat does not surprise him; it would surprise him greatly if we didn't; but the circumstance of the wine surprises him indeed.

And what, he wants to know, do we drink in England?

When possible, we say, wine; and the answer for him is surprise number two. His cadaverous face seems for a moment about to drop apart. I half-expect it to give a hollow wooden-sounding chock! and fall to pieces. The bluish fleshless jaws look for a moment detachable as they part in astonishment revealing a dark mouth that says 'Wine? You drink wine? You *have* wine? In England?'

We say, Yes, indeed, we have wine in England.

But not, he says, French wine?

Yes, we say, French wine.

Of what sorts? The best?

The best, we say. To impress him with this we begin to speak, in a moment, of the wines of *Châteauneuf du Pape,* from which we intend to go on and talk of vintages more impressive, but the words are enough; he is convinced that the English, or some of them, are not utterly lost in barbarism. If they can drink *Châteauneuf* it is evident that, after all, they must be human, at least in part. But his astonishment still lingers.

He thought we had no wine. He thought it

was impossible, like the meat and the sugar and the bacon and the cheese. Especially the cheese. He cannot understand the cheese; it is even more difficult to understand than the wine. I am not surprised he cannot understand the cheese. France produces no less than five hundred cheeses, of which some scores are famous, of which the majority are of local character and consumption, the product of her still virile peasantry. Fortunately he does not ask us how many cheeses we have in England; he would be shocked to learn that the answer was only one and perhaps in any case we could not describe it. Only a day later this one is in fact described for me – as if I needed description – by a young English farm-labourer, whose father undoubtedly lived very largely, before the war, on this simple staple food. He has been trying to eat his meagre prison-like portion of cheese for supper. 'But you carn't eat it,' he says. 'It's wussn bloody soap. It's wussn – God, you wouldn't give it to a bloody rat.'

But fortunately we are able to hide these facts from the Frenchman, who goes on to tell us, after he has recovered from his astonishment about the wine, that this coastal hinterland on which he lives, so close to the great rolling switchbacks of corn that make the Pas de Calais a place of almost noble agricultural beauty in August, is a region of great richness for game and meat and fish and good things. And so we get him, at last, to talk about the country-side, his thoughts turning to Normandy, a hundred kilometres down the coast, and his face, at the thought of that still richer, still creamier, more buttery region, losing for a moment its cadaverous melancholy and becoming illuminated with a dry, un-believing and not altogether unembittered wonder. Normandy is rich and Normandy is mean. They live well in Normandy and their spoils are under the bed. They roll in cream and they are grasping. During the war he would cycle, it seemed, a hundred miles into Normandy in order to buy and barter: cigarettes for butter, cigarettes for cheese, cigarettes for a joint or two of pork. All France was doing these things; and as he speaks, my mind begins to go back to the Maupassant-like farmhouse château of grey stone and pale blue jalousies with the servant girls sewing at an open window overlooking a courtyard at which, a few days after invasion, I stayed in 1944. It goes back to great square blocks of butter, to fragrant melons, to sun-black peaches on warm walls, and a dinner of beautiful excellence eaten in a solid smoke-soft kitchen where landowner, bailiff, governess and the rest of the profoundly French characters of the house ate, in the old manorial style, together. This was something that had gone from England with my grandfather and that now would never come again: a self-contained unit, as dead and obsolete as the strip system of cultivation. But in France it still survives, perhaps as stubbornly in Normandy as anywhere, making the country an eighteenth century country still, a century or more behind us with our intensive mechanization and yet in a human way still in front of us, in all ways more intensely rural and through its peasantry closer to the soil.

And my mind, led back by the waiter's talk through the rich orchard-and-butter country of Normandy, through a richness hardly affected even by war, came gradually full circle, to complete a thought about the country of calvados and the country of white clover. It had seemed to me often that they were very alike in scene, in their great and varied pattern of landscape and husbandry, and in the special atmosphere that rainy sea-climates give the districts of supreme fertility. Odd that these two counties, each perhaps the richest of their respective countries, should produce a people of most suspicious and independent meanness, each conforming so closely to the tight-fisted peasantry, with its suspicion of strangers and its hatred for those who break its rules, so well and so often described by

Maupassant, who himself belonged to it. More curious still, perhaps, that the effect of a kindly, benevolent, almost luscious countryside, producing corn, fruit, grass, sheep, cattle, timber and hops in such easy abundance, should so often affect not only those who are born into it but those who come to it by adoption. Scottish farmers, of whom Kent is full, come from the Lowlands of their own country to find in Kent, where spring is earlier and summer longer and winter less harsh, a state of agriculture that is almost paradise. Yet the new southern benevolence of scene appears not to breed benevolence in them. It seems simply to offer deeper soil in which native parsimony can root afresh, grow more stubbornly and endure much longer. Richness concealed by the pretence of poverty, a bargain driven with steely hardness, a determination to wrest as much from the soil and from other people as possible and then keep it, preferably away from banks, until the death-bed whisper of 'Look behind the dresser' –

these are, of course, characteristics of peasantry everywhere, and not only of peasantry. But when, in the restaurant overlooking the meadows about Etaples, our friend the waiter begins a series of reminiscences about the way Norman peasants had been caught with millions of obsolete francs at a sudden change in the design and value of paper currency, all the stories of Kentish farmers being caught in the same way by the calling in of five-pound notes come back to my mind. The only difference is that over there, in Normandy, the peasant survives and flourishes in flesh, in habit, in method and in name. At home we have, as such, no peasantry; we have only, fixed as ever, indestructible, imperishable even under the weight of grain-driers, harvest-combines, hay-balers, mechanical hop-pickers and the inevitable television set, the peasant mind.

We left the waiter, the meadows about Etaples, the swathes of French hay and the sprinkling nozzles of water on the airport lawns, while the evening sun was still shining. In the aeroplane the silk-shirted gentlemen, after a wonderful excursion consisting entirely of joyful experiences in bars, were in a state of high and not un-pleasantly bawdy gaiety. They had said passionate, demonstrative and most un-English farewells to several ladies of uncertain character behind the customs shed; their silk-shirted bosoms were filled, obtrusively, with a clanking collection of porcelain ashtrays, which were now and then bounced up and down in noisy imitation of female shapes, jellied and uncorseted. There was much loud laughter. They clung to each other's necks and roared, at intervals, under the force of hilarious reminiscences. Below us, quite unnoticed by them, the sea was of ex-ceptional beauty and calmness. It took on its unrippled surface of palest blue the entire path of setting sunlight like a strip of solid gently beaten gold, so that the sea did not seem to be composed of water any longer. In a few minutes England came out of the northern summer evening haze exactly, once again, like a piece of green-crusted cheese, and the sun, intensely fiery and molten, sank into the western sea.

In a few minutes more we were down on our native soil. On roadsides and railway banks men were burning hay; and at home, on my own land, the farmer who had been given seventeen acres of hay for nothing had still not bothered to cut it. Two others, too prosperous to worry with such trivialities, had already refused it and now, in a country where only six months ago cattle were dying for want of food, it was deteriorating rapidly to seed. We were home again in England – England with her one cheese, her free false teeth for Tom, Dick and Harry but little or no meat for Tom, Dick and Harry to eat with them, a land of burning hay and hunger and a stupefied, bewildered people wondering why.

10 The New Hodge

When I came first to live in Kent, during the agricultural doldrums between the wars, the wages of ordinary farm labourers were a little over two pounds a week, or tenpence an hour; the price of land was sometimes as low as five pounds an acre, and a large estate, consisting of several farms, a mansion, four hundred acres of arable, pasture and woodland, had just changed hands for something over ten thousand pounds, a mere fraction of its value today; butter was tenpence a pound, bacon a shilling and cherries, our rich, almost unfailing harvest of the bountiful brick earth, were generally not more than sixpence and often less; farmers were in a poorish way, ready to take in guests during the summer time or to bring a parcel from the station for a few pence a time, though one of them had just died leaving a quarter of a million, grumbling to the last that he could not afford a fire in the room in which he died; at a local mansion twenty-two gardeners were employed and gay parties were given at week-ends in a heated swimming pool; hunting was a daily and very popular rampage in winter-time and pheasants were everywhere as thick on the ground, in early autumn, as chickens in a farmyard; the poor complained that they could not eat meat more than twice a week and there were even rumours, at election times, that country labourers were not entirely convinced of the secrecy of the ballot system, as a consequence of which they often did not vote at all; a cottage cost five or six shillings a week to rent and as little as five hundred pounds to buy; you could pick up at the local market a second-hand car, true a little ramshackle but a good runner as the auctioneer would say, for twenty-five pounds; at the market too you could buy a chicken or a duck for half-a-crown, a plump young turkey for eight or nine shillings, and a rabbit or a pigeon for sixpence; down at the coast you could buy a fat little plaice, rightly renowned as the best in the world, for sixpence a lump, pick where you like, lady, fresh from the boats in the harbour, and a Dover sole of superb firmness and brilliance for ninepence a time. All about you the bountiful harvest of earth and sea was cheap and unspoiling, and on everybody's lips was the phrase 'the drift from the countryside.'

The impressions of the succeeding years are sometimes chaotic; they become telescoped into themselves, creating distorted illusions, the exact sequence of time and events difficult to remember and clarify, so that sometimes one does not seem to be living in the same countryside, with the same people, or the same economy. A curtain separates us from the 1930's, with what now seems to be their much overrated difficulties and bewilderments, almost as securely as it does from the eighteenth century. The wages of a farm labourer are now between five and six pounds a week and are to be further raised this year, and the motor-bike on which he goes to work or to cricket has cost him two hundred pounds; he puts in a good deal of odd job work, when he can, a half a crown or three shillings an hour, not a penny of which ever finds its way into those returns for tax which so obsess and oppress so many of his fellows in the town; he can still eat meat only twice a week but this unfortunate fact, once the fault of an economy that kept him down-trodden, is now the fault of an economy that in other ways has lifted him up; on the other hand a chicken costs him twenty-five shillings, a duck sometimes more, a rabbit six shillings and a pigeon the same; the fields are remarkably empty of pheasants and although the hunt, much thinned out and straggling, still hunts through the winter, he cannot eat foxes; beer is nearly treble the price it used to be and the rents of newly-built cottages are twenty-five shillings, or about half his weekly wage of twenty years ago; bread is still his staple diet, together with potatoes, tea, vegetables and an occasional slice of some gastronomical horror called meat-loaf, which is clearly neither meat nor loaf and of questionable value anyway; in the words of William he 'don't git enough in moi belly' and it seems plain that if he starved twenty years ago under capitalism he is not more than a point removed from the same condition under socialism today. Of his employers he does not speak with anything like the same reticence as he used to do, and this, perhaps, is not surprising; he sees about him a farming community that, to his way of thinking, has grown very rich. As one man puts it to me, before he proceeds to tell me that the stairs in his millionaire-owned cottage are propped by chestnut spiles so that they do not fall down, they 'git a subsidy for everything nowadays except bloody 'edge-cuttin' and 'fore s' long they be gittin' that an' all' – a statement quite incontestable in its accuracy. The land has been fed by a fabulous diet of subsidies, a condition in which it was possible until recently for a man to sell potatoes to the government and to buy them back again, all in the same afternoon, at a profit, without ever lifting a sack of potatoes on to a truck. He sees it not only fattened, or sickened, by subsidies, inevitable though they may have been; he sees it, on all sides, the prey of parasites. Farms have become a neat way of losing and yet of making money. The labourer, I think, it not embittered by this; but he knows it, notes it, thinks on it, probably resents it but, above all, in a way not possible a few years ago, speaks of it openly. He is aware of a new type of absentee landlord: the daily absentee, seen for a few moments at the close of a summer day or at week-ends. He himself is no fool, and perhaps it is simply in the inevitable course of things that he too, at week-ends, should play his own game of 'gittin' a bit out of it fer meself,' a game played on the not inhuman principle, once held up before us almost as a text, of the labourer being worthy of his hire. Indeed the not unsurprising fact emerges that the labourer, like the landlord, is only human after all.

He is also, because of that humanity, a person, largely, of remarkable loyalty. War has left his condition not very greatly different from that of twenty years ago: in some ways better, in some ways worse, but on balance about the same. He still eats meat only twice a week, though his wage is almost twice as large; his children are given government allowances and are taken to school in taxis but they miss, as he does, the joint of home-fed pork, the brawn, the bacon, the chitterlings, the lard and the ham; wages are everywhere higher but money goes like water. He sees, on the other hand, the bad farmer fattening just as easily as the good farmer, and both of them probably growing, in his eyes, rather meaner in the process. Yet his loyalty remains. In a country racked by strikes of incredible pettiness, arising from causes that the average third-form boy would regard as not worth the intelligence of infants in napkins, the farm labourer stands out as a man who never strikes, never blackmails or blacklegs, and is never locked out. Perhaps he never thinks of it, but it is my fancy that he knows, either instinctively or in his heart, that he does not simply work for man; his boss is a sort of higher system, an ancient and traditional combination of climate and earth to which he owes, and will always give, the deepest loyalty. It would seem to him a condition of supreme idiocy to strike against that, to default in his duty at those dateless moments in the calendar that are infinitely older than pickets and legislation: the days of seed-time and the plough, of harvest-time and hay. He is of course a great grumbler, but it never comes to much; it never smoulders beyond grievance into political flame; he still does not go with any great consciousness into politics; he knows that, in most cases, the guv'nor is a Tory, and he gets a good laugh out of watching gatherings of speech-making ladies gathered on country lawns, listening to Tory M.P.s, in summer-time, but it is rather the same laugh that he gets out of watching the local parson, outrageous in florid surplice and stole, floating to his empty church on Sunday mornings. His own parliament is still the local pub, his pulpit the saloon-bar. There he can let off steam of all kinds, especially against those too-earnest inter-lopers who are always arriving in villages with the fixed intention of buying rural favour or changing the rural lot, and laugh at this sect or that and in his sturdy, stubborn and admittedly sometimes stupid heart not care a damn.

During these years, when on paper his lot seems to have become much better but has in reality remained about the same, something of extreme significance has been going on about him in the countryside. The condition of drift from countryside to town, so much talked about in the early days of the depressed and foreboding 'thirties, has stopped. It has in fact, according to the newest census figures, been reversed. No longer, it seems, are countrymen forsaking country life for town life; but townsmen are turning more and more, as I have long prophesied they would, to the country. Such a condition, the reverse of something all rural commentators have been noting since at least the eighteenth century, is not an accident. It is one more inevitable result of the revolution in communications, swift alike in impact and result, that has killed for ever rural isolation and that now takes us, in a few minutes, to France for the day. By this revolution small countries, such as England, Belgium and Switzerland, have been more transformed than countries of the size of France, where economy remains a re-markably evenly balanced affair as between agriculture and industry and where great stretches of deeply rural countryside, poor in communications, separate the larger towns. It is probably this, combined with the fact that the pure peasant is a very much less malleable and flexible person than the emancipated type that has replaced him in England, that has kept France so much more a country where divisions between city and village survive so stubbornly and yet where the peasant character just as stubbornly survives in both. England is nowhere quite so affected by distances and quite half the charm of her countryside, admired everywhere as unique, comes from the fact that the pattern of rural and urban and half-urban is so tightly and neatly woven. And curiously enough much of that neatness has been supplied by the urban mind or perhaps more truly by urban example. In France isolation produces a remarkable rural tidiness, a shabby country sloppiness, that all travellers through its muck-strewn hen-scratched, unmetalled village streets know so well. Yet they are the village streets, near enough, of England before the revolution in her road communications, before the fusion of rural and urban and suburban made our countryside neater and cleaner and drier and more orderly every year.

Communications have in fact transformed the English countryside into a kind of everyman's back garden belonging to the towns. Indisputable though it is that the drift from countryside to town has been reversed it would also seem to be certain, I think, that there is an endless, fluid traffic, unassessable by any census, going both ways. We cannot assess the number of people who now enjoy, in England, something of both town and country life. Every village still contains its Victorian survival, man or woman, who over the years has never made a trip to the nearest town and, in typically stubborn or placid way, never wants to: a type well exemplified, for me, by a Kentish character who said. 'Whenever I goo Tonbridge and set my foot on the bloody pavement somebody wants to set it there afore me. Lumme if I wouldn't rather be up Smarden woods with my little dog.' But the type grows rarer every year. It is a long time, very long, since the English village was a self-contained unit revolving round church, pub, shop and great house. The great houses are empty; the churches are shadowy outdated survivals competing vainly with radio, the internal combustion engine and the deep disruption of constant wars in their efforts to attract something more than the interest of old ladies who still like to turn out, on Sunday mornings, as they did in the days when Sunday joints crackled in warm kitchens, in succulent pools of Yorkshire pudding, while parsons droned to the tune of sparrows chirping in graveyards. Great house, church, joint: they are all equal casualties of the British passion for engaging in constant war, and at least the first two of them, and unhappily perhaps the third, will never come back. But in their place, as happy consolation, we have the drift back to, and also the fluid drift in and out of, the countryside. That too has come out of war, and will remain.

11 Sea and September

September comes in with dark-blue gales and early mornings savage with thunder rain, with days clogged and humid as a bakehouse, the pall of cloud dark as January. Corn has lolled for six weeks in stock, a few fields of oats for seven weeks or more. Sheaves have the greyness and sometimes the blackness of old thatch and frequently, like old thatch, are sprouting sharp emerald at the beards. Grass everywhere is acid lush and green and on every acre of farmland, from waiting flooded cornfields to bright-brown potato rows, the bitter mould of a late wet summer has settled like sour crust. The trees are black as if they will never fade.

Now and then, for perhaps one day out of six or seven, the pall of dark grey humidity lifts and reveals, with startling acetylene glare, a sun of summery fullness and power. It pours through rain-freshened air with something more than benevolence for an earth starved of it; it stabs down like a jolting, almost savage injection of hot wine. Coolness, wetness, darkness, mouldiness are all suddenly shattered out of what had seemed a permanent grasp on everything. In a few hours dahlias begin to lift themselves out of drooping sogginess, to become again like spiky flames of scarlet and yellow and purple and sherry-gold. Fuchsias, never so beautiful as in clear sunlight after humid rain, are silver-freckled with tiny seeds of water that quiver as they drop or dry in the sun, and once again big grumbling bees begin climbing the magenta and salmon chimneys of the long tubes, fussing frustrated inside, helpless stupid legs entangled with the pins of rosy stamens. The tall white spikes of a most elegant flower, the Cape Hyacinth, in appearance rather like the ivory-belled stalk of a yucca, regain all their light, their quality of clean candescence that illuminates borders now grey, like the cornstraw, with weeks of rain. In a miraculous way begonias, their beautiful rich frostings of petals mauled by storms to the pulpiness of decaying scarlet and orange fungi, lift themselves up, turning new flat plates of flower to a sky that now has no more treachery in it than the eye of a child. Grass stops squelching underfoot like a soaked sponge and a few butterflies, so rare all summer that when they dance at last it seems quite miraculous, quiver about the browning buddleia flowers. More than a year of storminess, of fatal coolness and treachery and instability and rain, seems to evaporate and summer, all tender and warm and high-coloured, drugging like the softest anaesthetic, is back again.

Such a day, at this season of the year, and more especially after a wet season, leads us to the sea. By cross-country roads, really more lane than road, and nowhere straighter than the snake that only this morning lies under my very feet in the soft September sun for perhaps half the morning without my knowing it, we can reach in about an hour the Sussex sea. These forty miles are among the most beautiful in England, and somewhere half way across them Kent and Sussex divide. I do not suppose there is a more subtle division between Northamptonshire and Warwickshire, where a countryside of elm and hedgerow and grass and low-breasted hill seems to offer no clue at all to the change of county. And I suppose that in the same way a stranger making the journey from the heart of Kent down to the chalk cliffs about Hastings, taking in a string of small towns so much alike in feeling and style that they are like architectural sisters, Tenterden, Goudhurst, Cranbrook, Robertsbridge and Battle, might never know that somewhere just west of Hawkhurst he had crossed over into another county. Yet the small river that marks the boundary is always, to me, as sharp as a frontier. This is not an illusion arising from the fact that I know I am on the border; my eye notes it and my senses grasp at the subtlest of changes in the air.

These changes are not fanciful but have their origins firmly in the earth itself. Sussex is not Kent, in fact, because the soil is not the same. Somewhere about the border-line the soil changes; the richness fades. This does not produce suddenly a countryside less beautiful: but merely beautiful in a different way. Soon the hop-gardens disappear, and with them the great orchards; there is a startling decrease in the area of cornland, making you more sharply aware of how much corn Kent does grow, especially on the high wide lands between the superb cherry plateau about Sittingbourne and the sea; and with the disappearance of hops and orchards a certain grandeur goes out of farm architecture – there is not quite the massiveness, the church-like solidity, that makes the barns of Kent so much like those of Normandy. All the time the country continues to be very beautiful: all woodland and valley, fold with fold, with vistas of sudden green enchantment, under a sky charged with some subtle sense of the nearness of the sea. But the intensity of cultivation, the variation, the great fecundity, are no longer there. The landscape contains more pine, more bracken, more gorse and broom; the Sussex clay lies tough and unused on difficult little hillsides. There is no cherry-land here, worth five hundred pounds an acre, no benevolent blessing of brick earth. From a distance, to a strange eye, the pattern seems to be still the unchanged common southern pattern, field and hedgerow and valley and woodland going on and on until broken at last by sea. But the pattern is not the same, nor is the feeling in the air. A certain alertness, amounting sometimes to exhilaration, is missing. Fecundity is life, and life is worrying: but here life and soil are not so fecund, there is not quite so much to worry the sun-blessed rural folds; this is sleepy old Sussex – so sleepy and snoozy on the favoured coastal strip about Worthing that the air almost drugs the stranger – by the sea.

From such journeys, lovely though Sussex seems to us, we come back more firmly entrenched in affection for our own countryside, more convinced than ever that no part of England, the North and Midlands especially and even the West, can offer anything comparable to the pattern of things that surround us here. We have tested England from North to South, from East Anglia to the West, and in various cross-wise fashions, taking in every county but one. We return always with deepened affections, with conviction strengthened that, in beauty at any rate, the best of England is the south country, and that the best of the south country is Kent.

This opinion is really, as far as I am concerned, the judgment of an exile. I am a half-way house man. My roots belong not to the great jungle of industry and moor and mountain and pasture and lakeland, so much of it beautiful and startlingly rural and warm with life, that lies north of the Trent; nor to the county containing every subtle variation of landscapes and husbandry except sheer mountain and lakeland where I now live. I spring from the Midland plain, where habit and thought and speech and outlook are more profoundly and intensely English than anywhere else in the land: the country of Shakespeare, Dryden, Bunyan, the great universities and the established English tongue. North countrymen with their long and forthright vowels and west countrymen with their honeyed yokelese can only bow themselves out backwards when faced with the cradle of standard English that spreads along the green clay valleys from Warwickshire to the Wash, and even the south country, speaking a sort of semi-barbarous Cockney that is very cruel on the ear, can do nothing but go with them there.

Happily the beauty of the English countryside is not judged by the accents that are spoken in it. If this were so Kent, where grades of higher education appear to have so little effect on the general murder of English that you might well think the peculiar art of killing it so thoroughly was really taught in schools, would come very low on the list. For sheer plum-in-the-mouth doggerel, sloppy and bastardized, the speech of my adopted county takes some beating. Indeed I should be much surprised if any other county can offer such perfection in English misused. But if the ear is offended so harshly, the eye, the mind and the senses can only be continually delighted by the physical beauty of this piece of earth, two-thirds bound by sea, geographically, climatically and atmospherically so wonderfully placed that it teems with abundance. Spring comes to it early – so that sometimes I have gathered primroses by January moonlight here – and summer leaves it late. Its soil, notably on the famous ridge running from north of Maidstone to the sea, is not only among the richest in the country but also in the world. Its legendary cherry orchards are not there by accident, by some fortunate experiment on the part of an enterprising fruit-grower keen to supply the London market, but because its special deposits of brick earth, rich but above all superbly drained, are exactly what cherries need in order to grow to perfection.

Kent, more than any other county in England, is the most virile and beautiful testimony to the fact that the English countryside as we know it today, with all its special pattern of field and hedgerow and village and orchard and woodland and farm, is man-made. Where nature has been specially providential, as in Kent, this man-made pattern is bound to be of an intensely varied and fascinating kind. Here it embraces a variety of crops, a system of agriculture, horticulture and arboriculture, not to be found elsewhere in England, especially in the north country, and still more especially in Wales and Scotland. What we – and indeed the rest of the world – regard as unique is the English countryside, what we love most on the face of our land, the true England, is in fact largely the result of interference by man. Where man has not been able to interfere so intensely or actively, the result is different. Mountains are mountains, man climbs them; he does not and cannot attempt to re-shape them. The result is that you can walk down the valley of Glencoe or across the Snowdon range or a hundred other places in Scotland, Wales and the north country and feel, in the primitive and virgin bone of earth, that man has hardly touched it. Its remoteness, its poverty, its intractability, its barren splendour have all repelled him: 'Caledonia stern and wild,' like parts of Wales and the Pennines, belongs still to the countryside that warring chieftains knew and that post-atomic refugees will probably know, virtually unchanged in its atmosphere and shape since the start of our history.

Nothing could be less true of the south country, where husbandry has been pecking and scooping at earth's surface, with the incomparably charming results we see in Kent and also of course in Sussex and Hampshire, ever since the plough's first revolution changed man from a nomad with grazing herds to a settler with hearth and home. There is in fact a stretch of country here, extending from the New Forest in Hampshire to the great beech-woods that crown the North Downs above Wye, coming up through the deep hollied lanes of West Sussex, the great orchard-and-hop land of the Weald, through the superb tender-toned villages of Midhurst, Goudhurst, Rolvenden, Sissinghurst, Biddenden and many others, in which you will find scarcely a yard of earth despoiled by man. This once great forest, turned by man into a vast garden of which the supreme show-piece is Kent, is unparalleled in the country.

In my mind there is no arguing about this; it is so; and the greatest part of the beauty of this piece of earth lies in the ceaseless variations it offers. Orchard dips into cornland, cornland into hop-field, hop-field into chestnut copse; copse folds on grass and grass into strawberry-field and strawberry into flax; parkland and potato-land change to orchards of hazelnut and pear and black-currant fields; deep cut lanes of holly and hazel, splashed in spring with primrose and anemone and blue-bell, turn to neat tunnels of rhododendron. The land is a series of huge but gentle folds, guarded at the south-western and north-eastern end by vaster folds of downland. Nothing dramatic emerges. Hardly a single acre of ground has not suffered adaptation by man and through adaptation, over the centuries, become more beautiful. Peak and lake and moorland, with all their special qualities of attraction, have no part in a pattern that is essentially ordered and civilized and yet always, because of climate and fertility and the nearness of sea, wonderfully lush and free in appearance and to all the senses prodigiously rich and lovely.

There is no doubt that the sea plays a great part in this. It gives a quality of invigoration and yet of softness to the air, so that the days are nearly always without enervation. There is a certain bristling quality in the air, combined always with some subtle touch of sea-beauty in the light of riding clouds. No day is ever really sleepy. From the east the winds come sometimes with piercing sword-like bitterness, especially in spring, unkindly and dry and withering and horrible, white and keen as ice. But nearly always when wind turns and comes from southward or westward there is a wonderful sea-softness and sea-strength in it, never drowsy, never cruel, never really treacherous. I have no doubt that all vegetation, trees especially, responds vigorously to this atmosphere of constant sea-change, to an air so often drenched with sea-borne rain, strongly iodinic in quality, endlessly freshened. I would go so far as to say, in fact, that the sea, with its constant and tremulous power of impingement on two-thirds of Kentish coastline, is the power, above all others, that makes Kent what it is.

It gives the supreme touch of salt that brings the dish to perfection.

It is curious and interesting to think that London is the other great force always restlessly impinging, in much the same tremulous and invigorating way, on Kent and Kentish ways. For a county that really projects like a promontory out of London's heart Kent is surprisingly unsuburban; it lacks much of the stockbroker encrustation that covers the pinelands of Surrey and the river reaches of Berkshire. London had drawn for centuries on Kentish soil for its markets; the two have always fed on each other; and yet Kent has managed to remain, all through the process, surprisingly rural, with little loss of a vigorous and independent character. It has never become cockneyized, although the Cockney loves Kent, comes to its sea and orchards and villages and hop-fields as a man goes to visit relations in the country, and thinks of it, even more than of Middlesex, as his own county.

It is in fact still one of the nicest sights in England, I think, to see the Cockney coming down to visit us here at the time of hop-picking and apple-harvest. You can still meet him by road and, most surprisingly, travelling by horse and cart. Not so often, now, of course – but on the road about Swanley, on a late August morning, it is still a reasonably common sight to meet the Cockney family cart piled high with kids, bedding, trunks and mum and dad, all jogging down to Kentish hop-gardens for the month of hop-picking that begins on September the 1st. No other county shares this traditional influx of Cockney character, and only one other the special harvest of hops that is here, in Kent, almost a religion. Both Cockney and Kentish man come to it almost as to a shrine. There is a great family packing up and departing in all Kentish village families on September the 1st. Your daily help and your jobbing gardener vanish from the scene; children are kept from school; and the great business, really a sort of working festival, of pulling the hop-bine begins. A man and his wife and family may now earn, in a good season, with hard work, five pounds a day; a man or woman, alone, a pound a day. Both for Cockney and countryman the hop-harvest is a way of getting a free holiday, with something thrown in. Yet all the time Cockney and countryman incline to keep separate, both in the garden and out of it. The Cockney has his own camp, set up in the field, by stacks of faggots, the quickest possible replica of his own street in Poplar or Lambeth, complete with wives gossiping at doors, screeching infants, smart-alecks on racing bikes, astonishingly pretty girls, old prams, ice-cream vans, whelk stalls and a good comforting fog-up from cooking fires. In his own slick five-fingered way he takes a bit of the countryside and for a month or so makes it his own. The streets of superb little villages like Goudhurst become, on Saturday nights of September, segments of the Old Kent Road.

Cockneys have been doing this for years; yet they leave nothing urban behind. They come, hold court, turn modest villages into bits of London, drink their country beer and depart. And Kent, perhaps of all English counties the most stubborn in its resistance to invaders, whether from the continent or streets about the Thames, lets them go, having given nothing away. The thick rich fall of oak and chestnut leaf covers in a week or two the scars of cooking fires and the general mess of camps. The dreary little gas-tarred huts are barred up for another year. The Kentish countryside gives a sort of long autumnal sigh and lapses back into a beauty hardly touched by the invader, as if none of it had happened.

Yet I am convinced that it is precisely these impacts of Londoner and invader from the sea, resented and resisted though they are and always have been by the Kentish character, that give to Kent a certain sharpening of character it might otherwise never have. Because of them it has none of the true rural pudden-sleepiness typical of some East Anglian counties and of counties farther west. The farther north you go, in my view, the more insular Englishmen become; the more they resent London and incline to provincial jealousies of the capital city. Yet it is undeniable, I think, that London, hate it though we all sometimes do, is the absolute symbol of the English character and that because of it life in the south is broader, less circumscribed by provincial prejudice and less insular than life in the north. I think we even play cricket better here: not necessarily with greater skill, with greater cunning, greater intelligence or greater ruthlessness, but simply with a greater appreciation at the sheer sweetness and irony of the game. The two silliest games of cricket played in this island every summer are those between Lancashire and Yorkshire, both taking place on days known as holidays, where twenty-two gentlemen face each other on a basis of sheer stubbornness, without evidence of the slightest pleasure. This is only one example of how circumscribed the northern character can be and how impervious it is, in comparison with that from the south, in things that could re-shape it. The south, and in particular Kent, is constantly being affected by influences, both from London and across the channel, that it cannot resist and that make it less and less provincial as the years go by. And above all it is full of exiles from the north who never return.

Moreover not all of its beauty rises from its flourishing and splendidly varied husbandry. Man, over centuries made rich from wool and hops and corn, has left here a magnificent legacy of architecture, in particular of smaller domestic architecture, of cottage and yeoman house, and of barns that have the proud spaciousness of churches. Grace and strength, delicacy and solidity, combined always with an extraordinary softness of coloration in tile and brick and stone, have given Kent perhaps more famously beautiful country houses from the time of Queen Anne to the Georges than any other county. Village after village flowers in warm rosy sienna brick and tile, pleasant and satisfying in simple elegance. There is also a type of house common here and never to be seen in the north: the weatherboard house. It sits in a rich landscape more easily, more simply and more graciously, I think, than any other sort of English cottage architecture. The pure white or cream or sometimes pale apple-green boards lie in clean horizontals, overlapping, like the timbers of a ship. Indeed the whole structure and line of these houses has a strong maritime quality. With the double pitch of their mansard roofs they have exactly the appearance of painted arks, upturned. They are everywhere in the older parts of sea-coast towns and it seems un-questionable, I think, that fishing villages first devised them, building them naturally in the fashion of boats, and that the influence spread inland, up the navigable creeks of Romney Marsh and the eastern sea-coast, to inland ports that are now ports no longer. Where this maritime influence is strongest there are whole villages in weatherboard style, sparkling white, refreshing as streets of new-painted boats in summer. This clean lightness gives the climbing scarlet roses, dark purple clematis and the soft violets of wistaria a stencilled sort of brilliance, and in late summer massive bushes of rosy and ink-blue hydrangea sit with fat somnolence under the walls of warm board, glowing opulently. The essential simplicity of such houses has been raised to aristocratic dignity in towns that grew out of an earlier prosperity, such as Tenterden, Cranbrook, New Romney and Appledore, and in blandly proud little villages such as Rolvenden. Sea and seamen and sea-ways at some time touched them all, and the mark of the sea still remains on them, most of all in these fresh boat-like houses, many with tubby bow windows, most of them with the classical sash-windows of the Georges, nearly all with those high and fan-lighted doorways that confer on them the final touch of balanced dignity that is so satisfying and so enchanting to the eye.

It is Kent's great good fortune that the Industrial Revolution hardly touched all this. While the north and the midlands were being ravaged by machines and the grab for coal, while the miles and miles of back-to-backs, hellishly dreary in conception, execution and existence, were eating their way into northern fields, Kent was free to go on growing hops and cherries, corn and apples, strawberries and sheep, in the old sweet way. The continuity of the Kentish pattern is therefore almost uninterrupted and untouched. It bears astonishingly few scars, at any rate over seven-eighths of it, of what is known as progress. Fortune, moreover, continues with it: not a new kind of fortune, such as cotton gave Lancashire, but the same kind of fortune: the fortune from sea and soil and herbage and husbandry. This is the basis of its particular life and beauty and the chief reason why, if anything, it grows in beauty and prosperity rather than declines. Its richness is not something imposed from outside by changes of political, industrial or economic power: which is always, and now always will be, the richness of the north. The north has its richness and has paid for it: the north best knows how. The south, and Kent most of all, has had no price to pay for the heritage it possesses; its richness is under its feet and is continually blossoming, even in the shape of bricks and mortar. There is so little about it that is intolerable to the eye – I except from this the unpleasant purlieus of Gillingham and Dartford and some bits of coastline – that I cannot help wondering sometimes if one little gesture of industrial rape might not have its own reward in making everybody here more sharply aware of what exactly it is they possess in and about these flowery orchard-folds. But this would be rather like wishing an Australian drought on England simply in order to make Englishmen appreciate the wonder of rain; or a Jamaican hurricane so that we could all be more thankful for our tender, trying, temperate island air. Kent, happily, belongs to us all.

12 The Turn of the Year

As November turns to December and frost transforms dahlias in one night to flabby skeletons clothed in brown wet rubber, the first crocuses, the little species *Laevigatus Fontenayi,* which we planted in October, are already in bloom, tender clean mauve cornets, sparked with orange. They tremble in the west wind that is heavy with sea-warmth, opening in the mornings at a touch of sun. They are not only singularly beautiful in themselves, startling and delicate in pure pristine freshness, but they have the great virtue of flowering for nearly two months, until almost February, by which time they will have been joined and smothered by the many rivulets of purple and white and yellow and chocolate-orange of all the species we grow. There are ten or twelve of these species, about a third of the number of winter-flowering crocuses listed in more adventurous catalogues, and we try to add to them three or four varieties every year; and, since the first of them follows immediately on the leafless horns of the autumn flowering species that begin in September, we could claim, if we wished, that we had crocuses in bloom for six months of the year. But the autumn-flowering species, distinguished though they are do not seem to be crocuses in quite the same way as the species of winter and spring. Moreover they tend to rise and flower and die unnoticed in the still lush forests of autumn leaf and flower, whereas the first winter-flowering species come to bloom on bared earth, on a landscape toned down, darkened and made frugal by frost. They are the true crocus: so miraculously spring-like in the heart of winter, so insistent to flower all through the dark turn of the year, that they are, even more than the winter tulip species, the most precious of things to grow.

The species *Laevigatus Fontenayi*, a little more expensive than most others but so generous in flower that small numbers will give great riches in return, is followed by the even lovelier and more kingly *Imperati*, a sort of imperial variation of it, larger, more elegant and in colour having the same exquisite continuation of fawn and mauve as *Iris Stylosa*, which it precedes by a week or two. It never fails, with us, to bloom by Christmas Day and like *Tulip Kaufmaniana* it affords the double pleasure of being so beautiful when closed that it seems impossible for it to be more beautiful when opened, and vice versa. It combines a richness and delicacy, together with virility, that does not seem to belong to winter. In its exquisite slenderness it too goes on flowering all through January, by which time the full tide of all the species has begun to flow. Of these species it is never quite certain which will come next; but it is fairly certain that the many hybrids of *chrysanthus*

– they already grow in number like the hybrids of *Tulip Kaufmaniana* – will join *Laevigatus* and *Imperati* before they fade. *Chrysanthus* already comes in variations of cream, gold, primrose, bronze and white, and of these *Chrysanthus moonlight,* rich butter yellow, and *Chrysanthus E. P. Bowles,* deeper yellow with feathers of purple-brown, are both so beautiful that I am always resolving, and never affording, to plant an acre of them. With them comes *Olivieri,* darkest of all orange-yellows, joyously brilliant and vigorous, about the same size, perhaps a little squatter or fatter, or *Susianus,* that has on its orange petals the smoky stencillings of chocolate that are characteristic of many of the orange-yellow species. *Korolkowi* is for example so densely stippled on its yellow petals that it looks almost black when closed: a sort of lowered candle flame, smoky and dark below, spouting a mere tip of flame. None of these stippled species have the flashing wonder of *Ancyrensis,* otherwise called *Golden Bunch,* purest tangerine, so generous that it gives twenty or twenty-five blossoms from a single bulb, nor of *Aureus*, a pure yellow species without a mark. All these will flower in February, some of them perhaps in January; snow will even cover them in full bloom, embalm them and then yield them up again after thaw, fresh and refrigerated and generous and unbroken in their continuity of flower. Sowings of a most delicate species, leafless, needle-like and palest mauve, *Tomasinianus*, will always join them in February: perhaps the commonest and the most prodigal of the species, sowing itself everywhere, varying sometimes to bright violet, then lavender, then greywhite, never stabilized in colour, always most lovely. And then, at last towards the end of February but often in March, two species of supreme distinction: *Etruscus*, of a pure shining blueness, with flaming scarletorange stamens, abundant and fresh and shining as morning sky; and then *Vernus Vanguard*, why vernus and why vanguard I cannot think, since it always shows, with us, a certain reluctance to appear until the sun is strong enough to unfold the first *Kaufmanianas* and the first rose-leaves on the house wall. But its goblets of clear aristocratic French grey, touched with a faint inner bloom of Parma violet, give it a queenliness only matched by the imperial earlier beauty of *Imperati*. It crowns the winter crocus season with the purest distinction, and then heralds the thick concourse of yellow and purple and white garden varieties that the average gardener knows in March and to which he looks forward as being the first fires of spring, not knowing that he might have enjoyed, for a pound or two, a thousand of them, more delicate, more rich and more precious, since December.

We saw one of the first crocus of the autumn in Majorca, in mid-October, on the hills about Valledemosa. The blooms were deep pure yellow, clear and brilliant and startling under the shade of small trees of lemon and tangerine. It was still very hot and all about the valleys thousands of almond-trees were already leafless and the young fruits of the tangerines were dark and small and crinkled on the trees where the crocus grew. Everywhere there were fantastic and contorted olives, old trees bright grey against the rusty earth and then soft green-silver against the vivid and amazing sky. They were especially lovely above the little coves by the sea. There the land rises steeply from the rocks, and red-twigged bare almonds are laced among the great drunken olives falling about the slopes, backed by the intense moss-green of tufted pines and the blue wine-bright water.

Going out of a shadowy September England into those hot valleys, climbing up through cream-white villages fiery with bougainvillea and pale-blue hedges of plumbago flanking gardens of blistered corn, was like going back into summer. Dates were golden and small on the palms. Most of the vines were bare of fruit and already the olives were gathered. The season, people said, was over. Only a few respectable, solid, very well-behaved Spaniards, munching at mid-morning on three-inch sandwiches, concealing a smear of pimento and garlic about the size of a fig, accompanied us about the hot gardens and through the tiny monastic rooms where Chopin lived in forbidding paradise with the formidable Georges Sand. At mid-day we ate by the sea. Hot white streets of houses were shuttered by jalousies of striped pink and green, and the meal went on until three or four o'clock under an arbour of dried pine branches, out of the sun. Then in the cooling afternoon there were more gardens. We walked about terraces of old stone, listening to the light fall of water dribbling down through irrigation channels under lemon-trees.

Then, lower down, where there was no longer any sun, we saw the crocuses, flaming yellow, very beautiful on the dark dry earth. I picked a few leaves of tangerine as I stood watching them, smelling the scent of them while I crushed them in my hands. And in a moment the bright crocus and the sweet aromatic leaves, so lovely in the darkening garden, seemed to come together.

It was all so very un-English that I could not believe that in England frost might already have blackened the dahlias or that cherry-leaves were already copper and scarlet and falling on wet lush grass. The smell of tangerines lingered in the air. The crocus faded, and across the Mediterranean, southward, the sunset was splendid with deeper combinations of the yellow and orange of the fruit and the flower.

Now, again in England, in what people begin calling the dying year, these two things come together again. In the house, stronger even than the smell of burning oak, the scent of tangerines; outside, among the rocks that have in the damp winter air exactly the fiery brilliant green of the Majorcan summer pines, the first crocus.

The air is full of dark warmth coming in from the sea. The grass is acid green after rain. The parrot-green buds of forsythia are beginning to open on the house wall and on windless days bright red twigs of lime and hawthorn are motionless and hold a million drops of white water.

Thrushes sing in the half-light, morning and evening, and as I stand and look at the delicate fiery heart of the little crocus and then up at the bare branches of my only almond-tree there is a wonderful feeling of mystery in the air. Christmas is over. A few spared geese cry across the quiet fields, and the year has turned.

The publishers hope that this book has given you enjoyable reading. Large Print Books are especially designed to be as easy to see and hold as possible. If you wish a complete list of our books please ask at your local library or write directly to:

Magna Large Print Books
Magna House, Long Preston,
Skipton, North Yorkshire.
BD23 4ND

This Large Print Book for the partially sighted, who cannot read normal print, is published under the auspices of
THE ULVERSCROFT FOUNDATION

To renew or order library books visit
www.lincolnshire.gov.uk
You will require a Personal Identification Number.
Ask any member of staff for this

F

BATES

The Country of White Clover

£17.99

LARGE PRINT   L5/9